EMERGE

"Discover How to Emerge from Your Cycle of Excuses and Blame to Step into Your Purpose."

Barba   ard

Copyright @ 2019
By Barbara P. Hubbard
All rights reserved.

No part of this publication may be reproduced, stored in a retrieval system, or transmitted in any form or by any means, electronic, mechanical, photocopying, recording, or otherwise, without the written permission of the authors.

Limits of Liability-Disclaimer

The authors and publisher shall not be liable for your misuse of this material. The purpose of this book is to educate and empower. The authors and/or publisher do not guarantee that anyone following these techniques, suggestions, tips, ideas, and/or strategies will become successful.

The authors and/or publisher shall have neither liability nor responsibility to anyone with respect to any loss or damage caused or alleged to be caused directly or indirectly by the information contained in this book.

"Then David said to his son Solomon, 'Be strong and courageous, and act, do not fear, nor be dismayed, for the Lord God, my God, is with you. He will not fail you nor forsake you until all the work for the service of the house of the Lord is finished.'"

–1 Chronicles 28:20

TABLE OF CONTENTS

Dedication 1

Preface 3

Introduction 15

Chapter 1: 2 Old…Time Delay 23

Chapter 2: 2 Fat…Physical Appearance 53

Chapter 3: 2 Black…Nationality 68

Chapter 4: 2 Female…Gender Bias 86

Different Sides of the Same Coin 126

About the Author 141

Resources 143

DEDICATION

Before I can even image thanking anyone, I must give all Glory, Honor, Praise, and Thanks to the God of my Salvation. My Keeper, my helper, my joy. Thank You, Precious Father, for FREEDOM; You delivered me from me. TRANSFORMATION; You changed my past and used it to push me into my future. RESTORATION; You restored everything I thought I had lost, healed all my broken places, and restored everything the devil tried to steal from me. You gave me the strength and will to EMERGE into a warrior—strong, unafraid, and bold. You anointed me for this journey … because of You, "I AM BUILT FOR THIS."

* * * * *

Thank you to Deaconess Nettie Morgan. You were the first to speak possibility and encouragement to me. And upon seeing what you thought to be ability, you started developing, nurturing, and utilizing the gifts you saw in me. I will be eternally grateful that God allowed our paths to intersect.

* * * * *

Blessing and love to Susie Martin, my favorite aunt. Yes, I said it out loud. You have always been my cheerleader, friend, and confidant. You will forever hold a dear place in my heart.

* * * * *

Praise God for the divine appointment to meet and fall in love with Apostle Nicole Bonds. Your strength, apostolic insight, and motherly love healed a multitude of hurts and false beliefs. I will always credit you with saving my life and, like the spiritual mid-wife you are, birthing me into the real me.

* * * * *

Lastly, and most importantly, thank you to my 'babe,' my husband, Leon. You have been the loving glue that held us together, lifted me up, and pushed me forward. You are my first pastor, the head of our home, and the reason I love coming home each day. Thank you for catching the dream, running with the vision, and holding down home while I chased my destiny.

♥

PREFACE

Almost every day you hear someone say, "I just want to be me." So, here's my question to me and to you:

Who is Barbara? Who are you?

Am I really me? Think about it; are you really you? Can we ever really know now after being polluted by our surroundings? The constant bombardment of others' opinions on everything flooding from the TV, radio, iPhone, iPad, computers, and conversations all around us. There are voices everywhere screaming to be heard. Screaming to tell you how to best be you.

Sitting alone in my car during my two-hour lunch one morning, I was looking at the church across the street and verbally thanking God for keeping me up until this point in the day. This church draws me. As I work each day, each time I look out of the window directly in front of my work station, I see people coming and going, men working and building; some days, there are weddings or funerals. There is a longing in me to be over there. I feel like I have a place of contribution and spiritual maturing there.

I was thanking God for blessing me and giving me an abundance of love, happiness, and provision. I mumbled thanks to Him for choosing an unworthy vessel such as myself to be His messenger on earth.

I began to ponder just how blessed I felt I was based on my so-called "material" assets. That train of thought led me to reflect on my childhood of poverty and dysfunction (I'll save the dysfunction discussion for another time). I recalled growing up—the first 7 years of my life—in my grandparents' home. They lived in a small two-story, six-room house that had no plumbing, which meant we had an outhouse, and we had to walk to the creek or spring across the highway from us to get water for everything. I can remember walking down the path to the "spring," as we called it. We would each have two stainless steel water buckets. On the trip down, we would bang them together, making loud clanging noise as we imitated the sound with our mouths and chuckled loudly. The spring was a watering hole in the middle of a stream that ran down the side of the highway. We filled our buckets to the brim so that we would not have to make a second trip later in the day. As we walked back, the buckets would hit against our tiny legs, causing the water to slouch out, losing half of it before we got back home. They were heavy and awkward for us as small children ranging in age from 5 to 11 to maneuver. Condensation from the ice-cold water would accumulate on the outside of the buckets. As soon as we arrived back at the house, my grandmother would take the dipper we used to get water from the bucket and fill it with the ice-cold water. She would take a long drink, emptying the dipper, and then sigh with satisfaction and pleasure. She would say "Aaaaaaaye" and smack her lips. My grandmother, in my eyes, was a beautiful woman with shiny black skin and platinum gray hair that she kept braided in two plaits, one on each side of her head. She was strong and the keeper of the peace in the home. I can remember her making macaroni and cheese one day from crushed Cheetos when she didn't have enough cheese.

Along with my grandparents, besides my family of seven, there were two other families living there. An uncle and his family of four and my youngest aunt and her family of four. Each family had their own room. We shared the kitchen and the rest of the house. There was always some kind of joking or horseplay going on.

Still sitting in my car, I considered since that time how many decisions I had actually made and how many had been made for me by other people or because of circumstances. I had no choice in the parents I was born to, the home we lived in, the school I would attend, and the many other daily decisions. My mother chose what we would wear to school each day; she decided what would be served for dinner each evening and the television shows we would watch. As minute or unimportant as some of these choices appeared, still each of these determinations played a major role in forming the person I would become, the way I would process changes, how I would love and value others—and most importantly, what a healthy relationship with God should look like and how I see myself and place worth in the goals and dreams that were just starting to form in me.

Again, I asked myself, "Are you really Barbara, or are you just a product of your, his, and their decisions?" The word "decision" implies that it could have been different (good or bad). Even the slightest difference in any of these many decisions could have produced a profoundly different outcome. I thought about being in the grocery store, trying to figure out which line is the shortest because that is the ultimate goal, right? To find the shortest line and get out as quickly as possible. But what if my destiny connection is in the longest line, and because I'm in a hurry, I missed that divine crossing of paths? I missed out on the wave of ripple effects that would change my life forever all for the sake of hurrying home to the same old routine.

This gnawing grew inside of me, this wondering, this "maybe I missed it totally, and this is not my life after all." Could I be existing, and I totally mean existing, in a world that I was never supposed to inhabit? I imagined a scene from one of those Si-Fi movies with the parallel universe where each person co-exists in two worlds, living two totally different lives. On one universe, based on their choices and environment, they would be rich and affluent, while on the other, they would be living in poverty, fighting for their lives daily. Neither would be aware of the existence of their other self or life. That was the feeling I was fighting against. The feeling that I was doing the best I could based on the current circumstances but that there was a much better version of me somewhere else in my universe. There was a deep part of me missing and aching to find that me that was lost or maybe even dead.

Yes, this is me. Yes, I married Leon, and Tiffany is our daughter. We have the three best grandchildren ever; T. J. at seventeen is one of the kindest, most-considerate-of-others person you will ever meet. Trinity is a beautiful, fifteen-year-old that aspires to be a pediatrician, and Christina is our little "old soul" full of wisdom, six years old. I felt disconnected and detached from my current self; this could not be my life. It is the sum total of the decisions I made for me and accepted from others. It is what culminates after the final decisions have been made, and there is no point of retreat or return.

It is a good life! Hey, but suddenly, it did not feel like my life … my soul began to cry over the possibilities missed and lost, the opportunities unrealized and unfulfilled.

This was the life I settled for because of the "nos" that I should have said "yes" to and that "yes" that fear and apprehension stole from me.

It's the life that's good enough when compared to others. But how good is it in comparison to the me I was supposed to be? We always want to find someone worst off than we feel we are and say we're doing better than they are. Who are they? And how can or why would you want to measure yourself by someone else who is not the person they were created to be either? The measuring method has no value; therefore, the final analysis has no validity either.

Am I really me? I recalled Father's Day 2017. I surprised my dad by coming to his church for service, and afterward, I took him to dinner at Charley's. My dad has always been a man of few words. I guess that's where I got my introverted personality from. He drove because, well, he just liked being in control of his circumstances. When we arrived at the restaurant, there were some people standing in the handicap parking space talking. When they saw my dad turning into the space, they did not move. Boy I got scared and started praying silently because I just knew he was going to pull in anyway and make them move. Well, he did not; he looked at me and said, "Those doggone crazy people! Guess I'll just have to sit here and wait for them to move." Now, they saw him because they made eye contact, yet they did not stop their conversation or attempt to move. Mind you, my dad was a strong and demanding man that didn't take any mess off anyone. So, when he quietly spoke and waited patiently, I was thrown off. I whispered under my breath, "Jesus, the aliens done stole my daddy! Where is my daddy? And for the rest of the evening, I was kind of snickering to myself, having this conversation with Jesus about how He had changed my dad. I couldn't wait to call my oldest sister, first to gloat that I had our dad all alone for Father's Day and then to let her know the aliens had stolen him and replaced him with this calm, kind man that looked just like our daddy. After she finished being jealous about daddy and I being out on a date alone, she, too, found this totally strange and totally hilarious. This man walked, talked, and looked like my dad, but he had gone through a metamorphosis; he had experienced an encounter with God that had remodeled him, and were it not for his outward appearance, he was unrecognizable. That's what I was feeling. I was unrecognizable to myself. I wondered:

What if I had not listened to the voices of discouragement and negativity? If I had succumbed to my heart's desires instead of being so rational and cautious, then who would have emerged in place of this me?

What if I had used my thoughts and my words to express my feelings and speak up for me when I did not agree? But I was too timid and didn't want to rock the boat. Or what if I had used my creativity and giftedness to create something beautiful and new that is unfiltered by someone else's better way or better timing? They were in the same sinking ship I was, so what about them made me give them creditability?

Who would I be if I could have just been me?

Where would I be had I taken a leap of faith, or as Steve Harvey so often says, "just jumped"?

What would I be if I had said "Yes Lord" the very first time I felt Him tugging at my destiny?

Do-overs!!! How about a do-over? Hey, don't you see me over here raising my hands and jumping up and down? Can I go back or maybe start now? Am I so tainted and jaded by "you" that at this point I can never be the me that is really me?

When I sift through the uninfluenced part of me that is original to the plan of God for my life, surely this is not it. Now, don't get me wrong here. I understand and believe that God can and will still fulfill His plans for me. However, I do realize that I would never be the same had I made some different choices.

I found myself thinking:

I've succumbed to being less to make you more.

I've waited for my turn so you could shine now.

I've held my tongue so your voice could be heard loud and clear.

I've closed my eyes, held the tears behind the curtain of my eyelids, and put a smile on my face when I was dying on the inside. I was dying so you could live.

I said no to every opportunity, no to every offer, no to everything you should be doing, waiting for you to see the vision. Crazy, right? Expecting you to see and fall in love with a vision that had nothing to do with you. I now understand that I must nurture and cultivate my own vision. I didn't love me or the vision enough to protect it, yet I expected you to.

I lost my self-worth, my hope, my desire, and my me so you could find your you and succeed.

Is there any part of me still inside of me?

All these thoughts were playing in my head. My emotions were in heightened mode. I could feel my heart racing and my breathing increasing. I had tears running down my face, and my nose had started to run. I was in full-blown distress over what the devil was trying to plant in me, in my spirt, trying to still rob me of me.

I had to remind myself to calm down; all was not lost. Looking back now, I know God had to bring me to this point of crazy to help me realize that I was playing this blame game. He needed to shock me back to the realization that He is God, and nothing passed to me except it came through Him. And in coming through Him, He is sovereign, and nothing is out of control or lost.

Wow, I was on a roll. The pity party was on and popping. I blamed everyone and everything for shortchanging me and causing me to lose myself to this person sitting here before me now. Yes, I had sold myself out to everyone else's opinion of who I was supposed to be, and yes, I had not been brave enough to stand up for me. But that's exactly the point. The final decision was still mine; no matter how forcefully they spoke or how many so-called prophesies they had received for my life, it was still my ultimate choice to receive or remind them and me of the truth God had promised me through His word.

And just as I have had to come to see this truth. The truth is that I am who I am because of me—you to will have to regather all the scattered pieces of your life, all those shrapnel and broken fragments of your choice; stop the blame game and get back on track. Stop being stuck in that minefield, tipping-toeing around all the issues and mistake. Step flat-footed on the bomb and let the casualties fall where they may. Woman up and take responsibility for your own life and future. Quit wasting precious time and energy in the past and the what-ifs. Your future, freedom, transformation, restoration, and provision are waiting on you to show up. Surrender it and yourself to God and start making the necessary changes to emerge on the other side of this as the real you.

Revelation hurts!!! Still in the thick of my feelings, I thought they have gone on to live their lives. I've even helped them fulfill their dreams, build their business, restore their marriage, or make the next move in ministry. All the while letting the devil convince me that in helping them, I would be complete. I could live out my dreams through them. I remember telling people that this was my calling, to help other people succeed. And this would have been a grand statement if it were not for the begrudging, resentful reluctance hiding in my heart. That feeling of being overlooked and undervalued that kept me asking God why He always had me helping someone else fulfill their life dream, making their project better, and mine were still unrealized. My head and hands were all about the matter, but this heart of mine was far from it. Of course, we should help one another. There is nothing that we can accomplish all alone. If you write a book, someone must buy and read it, or if you start a business, there must be customers. In my self-centered mind, this thing was lopsided. I was always pouring into them. Then they would walk off into the sunset happy and successful as I stood watching their backside. They didn't even turn to blow me a kiss or wave goodbye. No "Thank you" or "How can I help you?" Just gone! And then when I would see them out somewhere, and they saw me first, they would try to look away before I caught their eye or pretend they did not see me.

This mantra played in my head. Who knows that the devil was winning this battle? He was winning until I got a lucid moment. A moment when I could smell it. I was setup. He knew exactly where to hit me to make me buckle and fall. He was distracting me and blowing this huge smokescreen to keep me sidetracked. Everything was right … it all happened. But I was supposed to see this coming and shut him down! I had just come off a week of fasting and a weekend of prophetic ministry encounter with 150 apostles, prophets, evangelists, and ministers, all fired up for God. I had surrendered all of me; I had recommitted; I had emptied myself and begged God to fill me with Himself. I shouted, jumped, prayed, cried, sang at the top of my lungs, and then here I stood caught, taken hostage by my own thoughts; I should have seen this coming. I allowed this invasion of my spirit to ease in and stay much too long; I had totally missed it. I was subconsciously expecting some kind of attack. But I was not expecting it in this form. He usually attacks me through my marriage and causes great distention there. So when he came out of nowhere with this train of thought, it was a sneak attack. I was blindsided and totally off my game. I did not have a plan for this. Instead of falling to my knees, I had fallen to the raw emotions, feeling of rejections and neglect and utter failure. I had allowed this invasion of my time and heart to once again rob me of forward progression and stability. I had been a part of a descending of God into the atmosphere of His saints, as we offered an outpouring of worship and praise. I left there thinking I've finally got this thing, I'm finally on course, and within a matter of a day, here I sat, all foolish and pitiful, crying over a life I felt I had missed when God had just shown Himself fully capable and sovereign in my life. I had experienced His anointing so profoundly that I couldn't sleep because I had to control my urge to run. And yet somehow I had been assailed, impaled once again. It was totally dis-hearting. I could not believe I was here, wallowing in self-pity.

A word of caution to each of you: The devil doesn't always

attack you in your moments of weakness. Often it is when you have come off of a spiritual high. In your moments of victory, when you are feeling yourself and have let your guard down because you think you are stronger than you really are, he eases in and wreaks his havoc in your life and mind. If he can get your mind all torn up, he's pretty much got a foothold.

Like this distortion of the truth, the devil uses many of the everyday things in our lives to waylay us and halt our spiritual and relational growth by getting us bond up in the excuse and blame game. We must remember that he only has as much power as we allow him (note to self). He has to get permission from God and submission from us before he can do anything to us. In order to arm ourselves, stand boldly against his lie and tricks, and EMERGE victorious, we must continue to fill ourselves with the truth of God's word.

In sharing my areas of weakness and defeat, I pray that God will use this book to help you see the devil coming and help you learn how to EMERGE from your cycle of excuses and blame to soar into your future full of hope and possibilities.

> *"For I know the plans I have for you," declares the LORD,*
> *"plans to prosper you and not to harm you, plans to give you hope and a future."*
>
> –Jeremiah 29:11 (NIV)

INTRODUCTION

We enter this world, and our parents look at us with such grand hopes, dreams, and endless possibilities. The sky is the limit; we can be whatever we want and are willing to work hard enough to achieve. But somewhere in the midst of it all, a new reality surfaces. We allow life to beat us down and steal all of our thoughts of this grand life of fulfillment. Disappoints, disillusionments, and distractions send us down a path that looks nothing like the vision we created in our minds. We develop fear, apprehension, and misguided anxiety takes over all those great expectations and big dreams and turns them into "what-if" and "maybe nots." We have our ideal college, job, and spouse all picked out. We have the plan all written out, and we read it over again and again. Years later, we find ourselves standing before the mirror, asking, "So why am I here without my college degree, married to this person I don't like anymore, eating Ramen Noodles?" The answer is, we let lies and excuses steal our plans, steal our life and immobilize us.

The Bible in Philippians 4:13 states, "I can do all things through Christ who strengthens me." We've heard it all our lives, and on the surface, we believe it.

I want us to not just read it, quote it in moments of distress, and say we believe it but to own it and live it out at every stage of our lives. It is when we surrender all of us to God that we learn to EMERGE into the phenomenal, gifted creation He destined us to be. The person that truly understands what it means to be able to do all things under His power instead of our own.

I believe a lot of things, but none of them move me to action, cause visible change, or affect those around me. I believe that if I eat right and exercise, I will lose weight and be healthier. Unfortunately, since this belief has no manifested evidence and has not evolved into any actions on my part, I remain overweight and on high blood pressure medications. This will remain true for me as long as I do not put faith and action behind my beliefs. And as long as I find more safety in the false security the excuses provide for me, nothing will shift. It takes courage and faith to step from behind the safety zone, face the demons of failure, procrastination, and fear and finally "EMERGE."

Emerging begins when we take the first steps to aligning our thoughts with what the word of God says about us. At that point, we can move from just believing with our head to reality, visible change in my actions and mental images of who I am.

At 56 years of age, I have unfortunately listened to the lies and made excuses based on those lies far too long. In my mind, I wasted 55 years listening to the lies, living the lies, and I now realize I've even found comfort in the lies and excuses. Because if I embraced them, then I don't have to do anything about it. I can just be comfortable with my simple, mediocre, somewhat successful life and keep suppressing the greatness that God so lovingly and purposely placed in me.

The problem with that theory is that when I stand before Him at the judgment seat of Christ (or bema as referenced in Romans 14:10–12, I Corinthians 3:10–4:5, and 2 Corinthians 5:1–10), he is going to ask me what I did for His Kingdom, and I will also have to give an account of how I used or misused the years of life He gave me. It's fascinating to think that God (who knew us before we were even conceived) has watched our lives unfold. He knows every move we have made. He knows our every thought, and the Bible in Mathew 10:30 and Luke 12:7 even says He has numbered the hairs on our heads. Up until this point, I had interpreted this as "He knows the number of hairs I have on my head." However, that is not what it says. It says, "He has numbered the hairs on my head," which means not only does He know how many hairs I have, but He also distinguishes one from the other. He knows which hair is hair number 2 and which is hair number 102.

That is so wild to think about. Having said all of that, my point is: do you not find it daunting to think that in the light of His all-knowing, He knows our heart, our mind, our motives, our every move before we make it and that He is going to require that we make an account to Him? This blows my mind, and I hope it will blow yours also. The thing is that accountability is not for Him; it is for me. So often we don't really know what we will do until we are in the middle of the situation. The only way for us to know our level of faith or commitment is to have it tested. Through these testing, we gain strength, wisdom, and ability

God does not accept excuses, no matter how well-thought-out they may be. So, the fear or should I say shame for running from His call on my life for Ministry—fear about the unacceptable excuses I've allowed to keep me from stepping up to the plate, trusting Him, and just being obedient—does not offer any satisfaction to Him or me. The light bulb finally came on, and I realized that my fear was misplaced. The thing I should have feared was having to stand displeasing and disobedient before God, not the fear of what family and society would think.

Well, hiding behind the excuses was working fine on most days. But every now and then, something would stir up in me that said: "You were created for more than this. You have a purpose; there are people waiting on you; you were not created to be comfortable and satisfied with the normal, run-of-the-mill, day-in-day-out drudgery of life. There is greatness in you! You are a 'Spiritual Entrepreneur,' and you are called to ignite and rekindle passion and greatness in other women. You are called to forge the way for others and to raise up an army of women that battle on God's behalf in the earth. A great host of women that, as they improve, also desire to improve the lives of others, find comfort in easing the suffering of others, and are able to see the beauty of others, no matter their current circumstances. Women that understand that they are an essential puzzle piece in the battle for the people of God. Women who don't become entrepreneurs for the money, but instead for what the money can do for the Kingdom. Sisters, salvation is free; however, ministry of any value or impact takes money. Women that know they have been called out to encourage, inspire, empower, and lead by their own example of integrity. Strong women that don't get caught up in the hype of success with full knowledge that any success they have comes from God and, by the same token, can be taken by Him. Great, creative women that use their creativity to build, produce, and establish products that inspire and uplift mankind. Women that have a tugging in their soul that speaks that this is something that must be. The Kingdom is demanding and in need of what you have to offer. It has been placed there by God for such a time as this. So, like Esther, we must rise to the occasion, EMERGE so that others can be spared and delivered even at the expense of your own life.

This inner stirring spoke that it was not too late, that God can redeem the time, no matter how much time I felt was lost and that now was the perfect time because I had finally made the decision to stop hiding, running, and making excuses. My heart was finally ready to surrender. I was saved when I was 9 years old at the Miracle Revival Fellowship Holiness Church. I vividly recall my Uncle, who was the pastor, doing the alter call. That particular Sunday, as He was making the call to salvation, it seemed like he was talking just to me; tears started cascading down my cheeks, and I couldn't stop myself from stepping into the aisle and going to the alter. Next thing I know, I am saying, "Yes, I want

Jesus as my savior," "Yes, I'm sorry for my sins," and "Yes, I believe Jesus died and rose again on the third day for the remission of my sins." So, my salvation was not the question; it was my surrender that was necessary. My letting go of me and allowing God to use what was already there. Those precious treasures He had placed in me while I was still in my mother's womb.

It is my desire that this book will dismantle those lies that you have allowed to take a root in your mind and heart and become excuses, that you will fear God more than you fear man and finally step from behind the hiding place and take a stand for the Kingdom of God. Stand up and be counted as a soldier for Christ. I want you to be moved from the excuse and fear stage in life to living beyond them on the stage of the life God created you to live.

I want to take you on a personal and scriptural journey that hopefully will offer you the comfort and assurance that is birthed when you realize that nothing of this world can compare to the glory we shall share with Christ when you finally understand your value and usefulness to Him. This conveyance can only materialize through knowing what He says about you in the Bible. And rightly understanding the Scripture you read. "Wisdom is the principal thing, therefore get wisdom, and with all your getting get understanding" (Proverbs 4:7).

We come with everything we would need to offer a full and committed service to God and His people. We are complete, whether old (time delay), fat (physical appearance), black (national origin), or female (gender bias). We all have purpose and a duty to God and our fellow sisters.

Job 23:10 proclaims, "Ye He knows the way I have taken, when He has tested me, I will emerge as pure gold." God, in His infinite wisdom, knows all about us. Our thoughts, desires, and intentions. He knows the wholeness of each of us and measures us by His all-knowing power, not on our human flawed-ness. Man does not have the ability or, for the most part, the desire to understand us at this level. Thus, when he has proved us by these frailties, in the same manner as gold is tried by fire, "I shall come forth as gold." We can find great comfort in that first; we have been tried. Tried for our benefit, not for any harm. But rather to burn away the undesirable or unbeneficial parts of our character. Second, that this trying is not unto death. We are not left in the fire to burn to death. Once the dross or undesired, unnecessary part has been burned away, He removes us from the hot furnace. This lets us know that the difficulty won't last always; there is a designated end in view. Thirdly, we shall emerge from the furnace like gold, pure and precious to the designer. We will be approved and improved.

Maybe you are like I was. Standing behind a wall of excuses and lies. Every step just bringing you closer to the wall, not closer to your desires or purpose. Stop bouncing against the wall in despair and defeat and instead "kick through the wall" and Emerge into you calling. You don't even have to kick it down; that's just another time waster. Just kick a hole in it big enough for you to get through; step through to the other side and never look back.

Emerge with me from the depths of excuses and fear. Soar high and look down on the beautiful life that God has prepared for those of us that will choose Him. See how He has used every incident in your life to create the beautiful vessel of God you have emerged into.

I pray that my openness and honesty will cause you to reevaluate your current position and make the necessary adjustment to come forth as a woman "SOLD OUT" to Christ.

CHAPTER 1:

TOO OLD "TIME DELAY"

"Youthfulness is about how you live, not when you were born."

–Kari Lagerfeld

"You're just too old! Your usefulness is all gone." The devil will use the very thing about you that you had no part in deciding and have no control over changing to put you in spiritual bondage so he can halt your life and stifle your destiny.

He wants to tie all your time and thoughts upon nothing so you're not focusing on that thing which will bring God glory and provide joy and even provision for you. If you are not careful, you will, like me, look up and find that years have passed, and absolutely nothing of value or substance has been accomplished. You have done many things; you have always been moving, but when you try to total up your successes and progression, there is nothing to account for all that effort and energy.

You must begin to understand that you are not here for you; you are here for others, most especially for the next generations of your family. If he can delay or even stop you, he has most likely stopped the next several generations. Some families never get back on track. They live under a generational curse of poverty, sexual dysfunction, and spiritual death. When the family loses, we all lose.

I love the idea of legacy, being able to provide a start spiritually and financially for our daughter and grandchildren. I like the idea that I can positively impact their futures with the decisions I make now. I don't want them to have to keep starting from "zero" when they can learn and benefit from the life we have lived. Each of you should be living a life with the reality in your mind that whatever you do has generations of repercussions. Proverbs 13:22 states, "A good man (woman) leaves an inheritance to his children's children ..."

What is God asking you to do or stop doing that has generational repercussion for the future of your children and grandchildren?

_____

_____

_____

_____

Have you come to realize that your life is not for you but for service to God and others? What are you going to change to make this principle a lifestyle?

_____

_____

_____

This realization was one of the catalysts that caused me to want to live the life I was called to and to be obedient to God. The weight I had been carrying for so long shifted. I still had the weight, but the reason for the weight had become the burden for others, an aching to draw others into the safety of the fold instead of the weight of the burden of running and hoping God would forget I was down here.

A mentor pointed out to me that just as the blessing of the father are passed on to the next generation, so will the failures and consequences of my own disobedience. She pointed out that my disobedience was holding up my daughter's spiritual growth and that my fears and apprehension were being passed on to her. She told me that in order for her to walk boldly into her assignment, I first needed to step boldly into mine. Just the possibility that I would cause harm to or delay my daughter made me want to do the right thing, no matter how scary or hard. Exodus 20:4 states, "You shall not worship them or serve them; for I, the Lord your God, am a jealous God, visiting the iniquity of the father on the children, on the third and fourth generation of those who hate me." And Exodus 20:6 states, "But exercising grace to the thousandth generation of those who love and keep My commandments." Notice what a wonderful God we serve.

He will visit our sins and fault to four generations; however, He will visit our grace down to one thousand generations. Doesn't that put the fear of God in you? So, no matter how old I am or how I feel I have missed my best years, I'll press on in Jesus' name because I have generations depending on me, and my sister, they're depending on you as well. I must remind you that your life and the good or bad of it does not end at the funeral. It will carry on in the lives of your family and those you have impacted long after your physical death. Don't let satan have one more victory in your life or "Legacy" because he keeps lying to you that you are too old.

Is holding on to that lame, untrue excuse worth losing another generation to satan? Silently confess before God; ask Him for the strength to move forward and reclaim your destiny and the future of your family.

_____

_____

_____

_____

Time delay and age had become my newest excuse for doing nothing. Girl, you're over fifty; you have a good-paying job and a great retirement plan. All you need to do now is to hold on for a few more years, and you will be living the American dream of retirement and traveling the world. And besides, you're too old to do anything new, especially in ministry. Who's going to listen to an "old" woman that has wasted all her youth and now wants to finally submit and say "Yes, Lord"? Understand me; like I previously stated, I was saved, but I did not want to be in the public spotlight. I loved being behind the scenes. If you needed it done AND done right, I was your girl. I didn't need any thanks or accolades. I was going to give my everything, and it was going to be fabulous. But it was not what God wanted. It was an empty, fruitless act of trying to offer an unacceptable sacrifice. Just like in the story of Cain and Able in Genesis 4:1–15. For many years, I could not understand why Cain's sacrifice was not acceptable until God revealed to me that that was me. I was offering something that "I" had deemed good and my best. And even though it was, it was not what He required of me. Sisters, stop giving God your supposed best and give Him what He requires, what is acceptable. Just as Cain had to reap the consequences of his unacceptable sacrifice, we, too, will have to. God is God, and He will not just take anything we feel should be good enough. We have to rise to His requirements—He will not come down to ours.

Although satan, we ourselves, and society may count people of age out and decide that they have no more use or value, God does not feel that way.

We have relinquished our thoughts and perceptions of what makes us valuable and desirable to the media, ungodly men's warped visual image, spiritually unhealthy women, and the lies of the devil.

Media portrays our worth in youth with photoshopped pictures of women with no wrinkles, pimples, or sagging skin. We see this so often that when we see someone older than 21 in a commercial or acting as a news anchor, we feel it is abnormal. Hilarious! We are so confused, and our perspective has been so altered by the false images on television that normal isn't even normal anymore.

I recently did a photo session to get some headshot to use for business cards, social media posting, and event flyers. When I got the finished photos, I didn't recognize myself. Every imperfection had been erased. They were beautiful, but they were not me. I went back to the photographer and asked if they could be done without all the retouching. She stated she could and said she has never had anyone ask her to undo the retouching. I told her, "I just felt like if I used these pictures of this perfect 21-year-old woman for promotions, and then this 56-year-old woman shows up, no one would even recognize me when I got there." I just wanted some professional photos. I did not want to pretend to be 21 again. As seasoned women, we should be proud to own all the imperfections that represent the struggles, the love, joy, happiness, disappointments, hurts, failures that have brought us to the people we are. We have endured them, lived with them, and sometimes look at the resulting physical scares in the mirror daily so we might as well love them and use them to propel us. Satan wants us to live a false life, pretending to be something we are not, all the while only fooling yourself because as soon as you show up, the truth will be known. And besides, who wants to take advice from someone who is not even comfortable being who they really are? When you become satisfied with yourself, then you disarm satan and take away the stronghold he has on you.

Getting Understanding:

Isaiah 46: 4, "Even to your old age I will be the same, and even to your graying years I will bear you! I have done it, and

I will carry you; And I will bear you and I will deliver you."

Here we see that God's promises do not cease because of age. God is constant in His care. He is the eternal and unchangeable Jehovah. He never changes His love or affections, nor His power and protection. He is faithful in His promises, true to His word, and the same God as we age as He was when we were born or first believed in Him. God has constant and sustaining interest and considers us valuable even in our years of deterioration. Just as He loved and cared for Israel through history, He also promises to do the same for the believer. God does not have a "statute of limitations" on the value of His children's usefulness as in common law systems. In law, when the period of time specified by a statute of limitations passes, you can no longer file a claim. We are never too old; the "statute of limitations" for service to God never runs out. He is always waiting, willing, and will not hold your delays and fault against you.

I find this comforting and reassuring to know that although I am reaching the downhill side of my earthly journey, I am beginning to feel less useful and that satan wants me to shut down and give up that God still deems me worthy and able to complete the race before me. He will afford me the same love, care, and prosperity. The prosperity that includes good health, a sound mind, spiritual enlightenment, and monetary provision.

I encourage you also to rest assured that you are not too old to offer God great service. Whatever your age, you are the perfect age. God is able to repurchase or retrieve the time that we feel we have lost. God can place you in the right place with the right people at the perfect time to accomplish His work through you. With one wisp of His finger, one whisper in an ear, or one seemingly wrong turn, He can set everything into motion as if time has no boundaries at all. Before you know it, people will be coming to you, want you to help and don't know why, writing you checks for ministry, catching the vision and running with it. In Christ, there is no wrong time or missed chance as long as you still have breath in your body.

A trusted mentor told me when I was expressing feelings of failure and laying blame as to why I had not been operating in my giftedness yet; he said that even in my time of making lame excuses, although it was not the ideal scenario, God already knew when I would say yes. None of this surprised Him or caused Him to try to work out a plan "B." My timing may be off, but God's timing would be perfect and without slack or delay. It is so sustaining to know that God can accomplish everything He initially designed me for even in my latter years. Psalm 91:16 reminds us: "with long life I will satisfy him and let him see My salvation."

Psalm 92:12–14, 12. The righteous shall flourish like the palm tree; he shall grow like the cedar in Lebanon. 13. Those that be planted in the house of the LORD shall flourish in the courts of our God. 14. They will still yield fruit in old age; they shall be full of sap and very green."

This passage is referring to the palm tree and cedar of Lebanon tree. The cedar's venerable age is measured not by years but by centuries. God loves us; we are the only thing that the Bible says "was created in His own image …" If He would value a tree like this, can you fathom the great worth and intricate details He has placed inside of us?

The cedars in Lebanon are immensely large, growing to 35 or 40 feet in girt and as much as 37 yards in the span on their limbs. They flourish for ages and remain green. When cut down, they yield a beautiful wood with brown colors that is solid and durable, often said to be incorruptible.

The palm tree is described as being constantly green and flourishing. It has vast wide branches that offer comforting shade. It produces a sweet, luscious fruit known as a date. The palms are considered an invaluable treasure to the citizens of hot dessert areas. Here, it is used as an emblem of the flourishing condition of a godly person.

If you are a person that is walking upright, a member in good standings in God's church that has been planted there by His gracious providence like the trees just mentioned, you shall retain your pleasant verdure, extend cooling shade, refresh countless others with sweet and nourishing fruit. "They shall still bring forth fruit in old age." Just think; the devil wants us to believe that there is no value in older saints, but God declares that when our natural strength fades, He will renew it. Our last days shall be our best days, in that we will grow in grace and increase in comfort and blessings. The palm tree produces minimal fruit until about the age of thirty. But, oh my goodness, after that, the older they become, the more fruitful they become, producing three to four hundred pounds of dates every year. So it is with us. Fruitful is the believer who is always progressive and whose righteousness increases as she ages. Who does not slack back but instead multiplies in service to God and care for others.

So, return to the original plan, that thing you have always known you were called to in your youth. Keep working, burning, and beaming more and more to the end of this earthly life. Don't give satan another victory in your life. Philippians 1:6, "being confident of the very thing, that He who has begun a good work in you will complete it until the day of Jesus Christ."

Look up and read each of the below Scriptures. Write in your own words what each means to you.

Psalms 71:18

_____
_____
_____
_____

Deuteronomy 34:7

_____
_____
_____
_____

Called and Qualified

If satan can't get you to keep running from the call to service for God, he then tries to stunt your success by making you think you can live any kind of life and still serve in God's church. He knows that if you are not true to your call and not making the necessary changes in your thoughts and behavior, you will be of little good to those you are commissioned to represent. He's counting on the fact that you will lose credibility with people as they discover the real you and that you will not have the anointing because of sin.

Age in and of itself does not qualify us to represent the Kingdom of God or give us permission to pour into others' lives. However, by normal standards, we should expect to have a reasonable portion of knowledge gained from our life experiences and education. Notwithstanding, the Bible has a higher standard as stated in Titus 2:3, "The aged woman likewise, that they be in behavior as become holiness, not false accusers, not given to much wine, teachers of good things."

This verse is loaded. So many are called and have said "Yes" to the call, yet they still want to hold on to the things of the world. Although again, age does not disqualify us from service to God, ungodly behavior does. While God can use us at any age, it is imperative that we be a vessel fit for His service.

As an aged woman and a woman called to impact the lives of other women, you must first get your own house (life) in order and behave as a "woman consecrated to God." The greatest portion of our service should be to the younger women of our church, communities, and homes; teaching Biblical, easy-to-measure, spiritually empowered, love-based living.

With another look at this verse, we see an example of a leader training or cultivating another leader as Paul instructed Titus to delegate the instruction of the younger woman of the church to the elder woman. Titus was the pastor; however, Paul was full of wisdom and order, thus he used this as a teaching moment for Titus. As godly women, we must be able to receive and give instructions. When we have that connection to God, that relationship founded in study of the word, we can then as needed provide a fit and timely word of instruction, encouragement, and even training for the next generation of leaders in God's Kingdom.

God has set us apart as godly older women. Women of faith, lovers of our husbands and children, reverent, wise, modest and commissioned us to search out and offer guidance to the younger women. To fulfill this great commission, we must first have mastered the biblical principles associated with being a woman called by God. It is difficult and, in my opinion, a lie to try to teach someone something that you have not gained a working knowledge of yourself. The old adage "Do as I say, not as I do" has long since gone out of style as a secular indictment to force others to perform in the manner in which we want them to. And more importantly, it has never been a biblical principle.

That "she be in behavior becoming holiness" conveys the

idea of priest-like. *Holiness* is defined "as consecrated to God's service, and in so far as they are conformed in all things to the will of God *(Romans 6:19, Romans 6:22, Ephesians 1:4; Titus 1:8, 1 Peter 1:15)*. Personal holiness is a work of gradual development. It is a daily restructuring of our thoughts and actions. It is a lifelong process. It takes specific and dedicated time and is a constant regrouping of our behavior through our speech and reactions. Looking the part will never be sufficient; a real visible change is necessary. Your testimony, the living, walking Bible will be the real evidence of what emerges from your commitment to holiness.

What an honor to serve as an "aged" woman. We are to live like a holy priest serving in the presence of God, letting our personal devotion to the Lord slowly influence every aspect of our lives. We are urged in *Romans 12:1–2* to submit our bodies as a holy sacrifice unto God for service.

Look up these verses. What does the Bible say about our bodies?

I Corinthians 6:19–20

_____

_____

_____

_____

_____

Galatians 2:20

_____

_____

_____

_____

What kind of "aged" servants would we be if we took these verses to heart and lived according to their teaching? Write out what your life of service would look like.

_____

_____

_____

_____

As a walking temple of God, a consecrated priest of God, a living sacrifice, and bondservant of God, we must present ourselves to the Lord as one having begun to live the life God has called us to.

"Not a false accuser" (slander). We can all agree or even admit that the tongue is the hardest member of the body to control. (*James 3:3–6*). So many times, the Holy Spirit has spoken in my spirit about something I'm about to say, and for lack of control, or because I think this needs to be said, and since no one else will address it, I let the "I will syndrome" take control of me, and I'll speak it anyway. One of my friends is known for not being able to keep a secret. When caught and challenged, she always says, "I have the right to remain silent, but I don't have the ability." Does that sound just like you or someone you know? If you really think about her, it is not her fault for revealing the secret but rather our fault for continuing to tell her. For some crazy reason, we value people's feelings more than we value their souls. We must learn to speak the truth in love and let God handle the outcome.

Although this is a universal problem, Paul speaks with a great indictment to "aged" women who want to serve in Christ's church to guard their tongues. A loose and profane tongue can undo or destroy your testimony *(I Timothy 3:11)*. The people you lead or mentor must first learn to trust you as a confidant before they will confide their hurts, fears, disappoints, sins, and even their joy, happiness, and blessings to you.

A tongue out of control speaks of a life out of control and can result in mighty destruction. The Bible in Proverbs 6:2 states, "Thou art snared with the words of thy mouth, thou art taken with the words of thy mouth." In order to have a life that is well ordered, we must first get control of our speech. We must learn to speak that which is Holy and in line with what God says. We cannot speak doubt and fear and expect to receive blessings from God. If we say we have faith, then our actions and communications should represent that as well. Proverbs 18:20–21 also mentions the power of the tongue: "A man's stomach shall be satisfied from the fruit of his mouth; from the produce of his lips he shall be filled. Death and life are in the power of the tongue, and those who love it will eat its fruits." Simply saying, you have the power to determine the direction of your life based on the words you speak. And in so speaking, because we speak what we feel is the truth, you will be governed by those words and will have to endure the consequences of them. So, if you want greatness and prosperity, then that is what you must speak. However, if you continue to speak doubt, fear, and negativity, that is what you will get. I think it is a simple choice considering the outcome.

John Barnett in his sermon *Being the Titus 2 Woman* says, "The source of all wickedness, especially of the uncontrolled tongue, is hell; and it is satan who is at the root of all gossip, all harmful talk, and all slander. If you are damaging the reputation and ministry of others with your words, you are a tool of the devil." You are a weapon of mass destruction, an uncontrolled wrecking ball destroying anything that happens to be in your path without any discretion or selection. So many times, like the wrecking ball, we destroy things that were not even a part of our fiery. They just happen to be in the line of fire or in the wrong place at the wrong time, and because you reached the point of uncontrollability, and you no longer care, innocent people get ruined or crushed by your poisonous raging.

The Godly, surrendered "aged" woman should never surrender her tongue to the devil but instead be prompted by the Holy Spirit to assure that what you have to say is completely true, honest, just, pure, lovely, and of good report before saying it (Phil 4:8). Don't let this character flaw recuse you and make your ministry ineffective.

How can failure to control your tongue destroy friendships, business connections, or ministry?

_____
_____
_____
_____

Some people believe that if you are thinking about it, you might as well say it. Do you agree or disagree?

_____
_____
_____
_____

Why?

_____
_____
_____
_____

Do you always have to be heard and not allow others to speak?

_____
_____
_____
_____

Look at these scriptures. Write a brief summary of each one.

Proverbs 17:28

_____

_____

_____

_____

Proverbs 29:20

_____

_____

_____

_____

Proverbs 12:15

_____

_____

_____

_____

Ephesians 4:29

_____

_____

_____

_____

Proverbs 3:1-12

_____

_____

_____

_____

There are many other Scriptures that deal with controlling our tongue and speech. With so much time and instruction given to this area, we must realize the importance of what we say.

Aged women are to be reverent in demeanor and not enslaved by much wine. ("Not given to much wine.") The key term associated with this translation is the Greek word "douloo." To clarify, let's look at some other places in the Bible where "douloo" is used. For instance, in Acts 7:6, it is translated "bondage." Peter used this word in 2 Peter 2:19 when he described the "bondservants of corruption." Paul used it twice in Rom. 6 to describe "servants of righteousness" (verse 18) and "servants of God" (Rom. 6:22). It is wrong for Christians to be slaves to alcohol or anything else that is addictive. *I feel a need to clarify here. So often people try to use the letter of what you say as a license of excuse or justify their bad behavior or actions. Instead of hearing the whole truth of a statement, they use it out of context of the full discussion because they think they hear a loophole. This is not a loophole. Please understand that this is not a license to drink what you consider an amount of alcohol that is less than an addictive amount.* Although we are dealing with alcohol here, it is just as much of a character flaw or sin to overreact, overshop, exercise excessively, etc. We tend to want to point our fingers at others and judge their shortcoming since our transgressions are not so obvious or readily seen. All sin is sin.

Driving home from work the other day, I saw a sign in front of a church that read, "Don't' judge other people's sins because they sin differently than you." Doesn't that totally cap it off? We love thinking "My stuff doesn't sink as bad as yours." Don't let drunkenness eliminate you from the service God planted in you. Be careful to ask God to help you judge your own life and to not get side-tracked by judging others. Remember that the devil wants you all tied up in someone else's mess so that you are not actively dealing with your own. Overlooking sin or being so-called too busy dealing with others will NOT be an acceptable excuse. The Williams Brothers, a great gospel quintet of the '90s, sang a song that has a line that goes like this: "Sweep around your own front door before you try to sweep around mine." Another line says, "Take six months to mind your own business and six months to leave mine alone." It's a catchy song that gets stuck in your head. But doesn't this just sum up the control we should have over our tongues, thought, and deeds when it comes to being an aged woman with discernment? That one sip is not worth ruining your testimony.

This verse concludes with saying aged women should be "teachers of what is good and train the young women." My Lord, my Lord, what a wonderful world this would be if we would take our rightful place as teachers of the younger woman instead of trying to be their friend, sister, and equal. We are not equal. We have a greater burden since we have had many years to learn and practice God's word and commandments. With this burden comes the responsibility to impart life-giving knowledge. We are to provide Bible-based, beneficial instructions that instill a pattern of good works. Teach sacred behavior such as good attitude, proper appearance, and the performance of service to the church community and in the home. The older generation as a whole is responsible to teach the next generation by word and actions. This is how values are passed from generation to generation.

If satan can keep us doing the wrong things, thinking the wrong thoughts, and championing the wrong causes, he can keep us from taking our rightful place on earth and in the Kingdom. Choose with me to no longer listen to or accept the lies or make the excuse. We have greatness and possibility in us.

The devil is a slanderer and deceiver. But we can find truth and freedom in God's word. Even when we feel that it's all over and done with—when we have prayed, fasted, and patiently waited—and nothing seems to be happening, God is working behind the scenes. Sometimes it looks like all signs of life are gone, everything has withered and died. Then by the mercy, grace, and favor of God, He breathes His breath of life into us again. We EMERGE stronger, more committed, and ready to run on to see what the future holds.

We can be encouraged by the life of Elizabeth. She was blameless, yet she was barren. Old testament law explicitly stated that those who are obedient to God's ordinances would not be barren. "[12] If you pay attention to these laws and are careful to follow them, then the Lord your God will keep his covenant of love with you, as he swore to your ancestors.[13] He will love you and bless you and increase your numbers. He will bless the fruit of your womb, the crops of your land—your grain, new wine, and olive oil—the calves of your herds and the lambs of your flocks in the land he swore to your ancestors to give you. [14] You will be blessed more than any other people; none of your men or women will be childless, nor will any of your livestock be without young" (Deut. 7:12-14, NIV). She had done all she was supposed to do; she had the promise, but she did not have the child.

If you are like me, sometimes you talk too much, telling others about what God has promised to do for you or sharing the vision and plans He's placed in your hearts because of your great excitement and anticipation. You keep talking about it, and yet there is no evidence of it. Elizabeth had the promise, yet she had no visible evidence of it. So it will be with us sometimes. We must receive and have faith in the promise even when the signs are nonexistent. Even when we think it has passed the time and surely will not come to pass. We must be reminded of the words in Philippians 6:1 (KJV), "Being confident of this very thing, that He which hath begun a good work in you will perform it until the day of Christ." The NIV Bible puts it like this: "And I am certain that God, who began the good work within you, will continue His work until it is finally finished on the day when Christ Jesus returns." My Sister, if we could just wrap our minds around that one verse, we would save so much worry and anxiety about our futures. God does not half-do anything. He doesn't get in the middle and quit or decide, "Maybe this was not a good idea; I need to rethink this and pray about a better solution." He is a better solution. We can rest assuredly in His plans.

As we continue to look at Elizabeth, we can't help but notice that she was well beyond the so-called childbearing age. Again, she had this promise from God. We, too, must learn to lean on the promise and the promise keeper rather than looking at our situation. It is when we lose sight of God that we start to see things in the natural; doubt can creep in, and we have the audacity to begin trying to fix things on our own. "I know God said this. I know He placed this in my spirit. He must want me to do something to help this to happen." Spoiler alert; God does not need our help with anything. We need only to submit and obey. Oh, yeah, and maybe have some serious patience!

Are you believing God for a promise, and it seems like it has been too long to come to pass? Repent and ask God to forgive you for doubting Him. Often times we feel that we have given our best and walked according to God's commandments, and yet we find ourselves not producing the promise. Search your heart and life for inconsistences and area of unconfessed sin. Make confession before God. Give the devil no ground to hinder your blessing

---

Amen!

Just as God birthed the promised child in Elizabeth in her old age—at an age that spoke barrenness and unfruitfulness—He can and will do the same in our lives. Age and time mean nothing to the creator of the universe. Our best days are ahead ... our most fruitful season is yet to come. I can say that because God has shown me in the spirit what my future looks like, and it blows my mind. There is nothing in my past that can compare to what's ahead. Legacy and provision for 1000 generations will be birthed through my obedience. I know if it does not happen, it is not because of the promise or the promise keeper; it is because of me. And dear sister, I don't plan on missing another thing. I serve notice on the devil that I am all in until the end.

Fine Wine and Cheese

We have all heard the ancient saying that wine and cheese get better with age. So it is with us when we are living in accordance with the word and will of God for our lives. As we age, we should be developing, growing, maturing, and ripening into new spiritual beings. The aging (maturing) process for cheese starts once the curds have been salted. Mathew 5:13 states, "You are the salt of the earth. But if the salt loses its saltiness, how can it be made salty again? It is no longer good for anything, except to be thrown out and trampled underfoot." So, no, devil ... we no longer see age as a disadvantage but instead as a great asset. An asset because we have been salted, tested, tried, and proven fit by the grace of God. Because we have invested in ourselves and those around us, we have great wisdom, knowledge, and understanding. We have made the choice to use all that God has planted in us to serve others and build up His Kingdom.

Buried Treasure

We've all seen the movies and heard the tale of buried treasure. You know how it works; you have the map; all you have to do is follow the map to where "X" marks the spot. Dig deep into the earth, and there lies your fortune. Gold, silver, diamonds, rubies, coins, etc.

Can I purpose to you that there is a greater treasure that is buried? I was thinking about all the things God has instilled in each of us. Knowledge, skills, abilities, trades, resources, books, businesses, etc. We have all these treasures that we don't consider as valuable. But they are. They a valuable beyond measure.

I mentioned early how I love the concept of legacy. All of these things are our legacy. A legacy that is much more valuable than money, home, cars, and fine jewelry. All of those material things will fade away at some point or be sold. But the knowledge and skills that God has planted in us or allowed us to acquire are incorruptible if we pass them on to the next generation. Do you understand how far ahead they can be if we impart these treasure in them, if we share the generations of wisdom—great-grandma, grandma, mama, you, and so on? All that treasure perpetuating itself. One generation building on the generation before, each adding and multiplying over and over again. The compounding interest effect.

When we die, our material accomplishments will die with us for the most part. But if you invest in your next generation or some young woman God sends your way, those things will live on. All those life experiences, if passed on, can become a living legacy. Don't take your talents and giftedness to the grave. Make a conscious decision to invest in someone else by sharing that which you have learned.

The devil knows the impact and empowerment we have housed in us. He is trying with every force of evil he can to make us feel discredited and ineffective.

As aged women, we need to remember that no woman is an island. We did not get to this point in time at whatever level of success you think you have by ourselves. God has placed people all along our path to sow into us. Your mother and father, a special auntie, a teacher, your boss, or girlfriends. All along the journey, there have been people pouring into you and investing their time and energy. And now it is our turn. I'll take it one step further and say it is our duty, our reasonable service back.

This is a great part of being blessed to reach an older age. You can look back and recall all the help and prayers we receive to bring us through difficult times. Without others sharing their experiences and gifts with us, where would we be? I remember a wonderful little old lady from my husband's home church, how she would encourage me as a young bride. She would always tell me stories about her marriage and things that she found that worked in her relationship to make a husband feel respected. She once told me to always thank my husband when he did something for me. She said, "Even if it was his duty to do it, still thank him. A man needs to feel needed and appreciated," she would say. "You can make him feel it, or someone else will." I took that to heart, and to this day, I thank Leon for everything. And just like she said, it has made a stronger relationship.

What is really powerful is to think of all the people that you don't realize are impacting you or even all the people you don't realize that you are impacting. Every lesson is not always planned or intentional. We will catch positive and negative influences from the people you are around. It is so important to be a person of integrity at all times, to speak positively and offer encouragement.

Understand your true value. Remember that it is not acquired just for you. Invest, impart, and transfer all that God has stored in you. Pour all that God and the year have given you into someone else. There is no return on your efforts if you hide your money under the mattress or bury it in the ground. We had an uncle that kept all of his money at home because he did not trust the banking system. He told one of my brothers-in-law where to find the money in the event of his death. Well, he died, and my brother-in-law went to recover the money. It was supposed to be hundreds of thousands of dollars, his life savings. He had buried it in the ground in five-gallon buckets and tin cans. Needless to say, when they dug up the container, the contents had rotted and molded. It was like a green mud heap. All that money was gone. He had spent his life accumulating this wealth.

Saving and doing without trying to leave an inheritance to his favorite nephew. But because of a lack of understanding and fear, in the end, it all amounted to nothing. Don't store your spiritual treasures where they can become rotten and molded. Be wise and deposit them in the empty bank vaults of women waiting for and desiring it.

> *"Age is a case of mind over matter. If you don't mind, it doesn't matter."*
>
> –Mark Twain

The Never "too old" Hall of Fame

Poppy Bridger, Owner of Anaheim Test Labs

After working as a Ph.D. chemist for 45 years, Poppy Bridger retired at the age of 69 to care for her ailing mother. But her 72nd birthday gift was an opportunity to buy and operate the lab she had worked at. With about $250K in savings, back to work she went!

On any given day, you will find Bridger testing the authenticity of a precious heirloom or analyzing the properties of metal fatigue. To help with the growing workload at the lab, she has subsequently hired her son and daughter to work with her.

She goes to work every day and, at the age of 84, is bringing into the business about $350K annually.

Barbara Miller, Founder of <u>Miller Paper Company</u>

Being an entrepreneur was never really a consideration in Barbara Miller's life. After quitting her job in the paper industry after 30 years of service, she assumed she was done. But as she packed her stuff, her former colleagues begged her to start a new business ... so she did.

In January of 1995, Miller opened the doors to Miller Paper Company and started with $300K in savings and 15 employees. Today, the business is generating over $7M in annual revenue and has been on D&B's list of the nation's fastest-growing companies.

The business has not been a walk in the park, to say the least. Miller started her company and was immediately sued by her former employer. A few months later, she struggled with ovarian cancer.

Sylvia Lieberman, aged 91. Creator of *Archibald Mouse Books*

Sylvia Lieberman became an entrepreneur in the fall of 2007 when she was 90. This was when she realized her dream of having her first children's book published. So, why not start a company to author and promote the book?

Archibald's Swiss Cheese Mountain is an award-winning book about a little mouse with a big heart who teaches children how to reach their big dreams. Not only is she an entrepreneur but a philanthropic one! A portion of the proceeds goes to two children's charities.

Despite her age, Sylvia works tirelessly, promoting her book at book-signings and readings, TV appearances, radio and print interviews, and even appeared on a float in a parade. And all these efforts increase the amount she donates to charities.

Time in Prayer:

Dear God, thank You for choosing me for Your service. I surrender my heart and life to You. Help me to not look at my age as man does but to instead see myself as You see me; fit and able to serve. Thank You that You will accomplish a great and wonderful work for Your Kingdom through me. Amen.

CHAPTER 2:

"TOO FAT" PHYSICAL APPEARANCE

"I am short, fat and proud of that!"

–Winnie the Pooh

OM goodness! I think I was born fat. Well, not so much fat as thick. My daughter, Tiffany, always says, "Ma, you are not fat; you are just thick, and thick is in vogue" What she forgot to do is to tell the rest of the world that her mama is just thick, and she is in vogue right now.

Although looking back now, I was not fat then. Now 71 lbs. later, I am definitely fat. I must also admit that there were times when it was a convenient excuse. I could just hide behind all that weight and an a-lined black dress, stand quietly in the background, and hopefully, no one would notice. They could definitely see me—but they didn't need to acknowledge that I was there.

I had allowed the devil to convince me that the world did not care what an old, fat woman thought, and it definitely was not about to waste one second listening to her. I imagined them saying, "If she can't even control her weight, how is she going to offer me any advance or wisdom on anything?" Through the study of God's word, I had to realize that none of us is in a state of perfection. It now amazes me how caught-up I was in my size. Looking back to then and looking around me now, more of the world is overweight than not. Most of us have fallen prey to the good life and all the food items that are available 24 hours a day now, and that can be up-sized with 3 times the calories we should be taking in for the whole day, let alone one meal. Praise God; He uses the fat and imperfect to work His perfection through.

I would walk into a room and say, "Girl, you really are the 'elephant' in the room." Weight is one of those things that you can kind of camouflage with the right outfit and some good contouring make-up, but you can't totally hide. It is for all intended purposes an outward expression of a greater inner battle. Everyone is fighting some type of internal battle that manifests themselves in many ways. However, most of them can be hidden, disguised, or lied about. But weight is just out there for everyone to see and judge. People look at you and pass all kinds of judgments about why you are overweight.

I have food allergies and food intolerance that cause me all kinds of discomfort and distress. I'm allergic to shellfish, beef, pork, tomatoes, and several medications. Because of intolerances, I don't digest well raw vegetables and fruit; I can't tolerate milk or any other dairy products, and to top it off, I have GERD, which means no spicy foods. Due to my diverticulosis, I can't have anything with seeds and nuts. And thanks to my IBS (irritable bowel syndrome), everything gives me diarrhea. Now, any reasonable person would assume that I would be pencil-thin; however, that is not the case. I have just found all the food I can eat, and I eat them. Thank God for Chicken; I eat it three times a day in some form on most days. Unfortunately, all of the things that I do tolerate are high in carbs like potatoes, pasta, and bread. Even still, I could limit the amount I eat and maintain a healthy weight. Life will always be about choices. And we can choose to let weight or personal appearance be an excuse, or we can stand tall in our assignments and EMERGE into amazing creations God is calling us to be. I like the thought of being "amazing."

I can remember going through the family lineage, trying to defend my obesity by telling myself and sometimes others that I shouldn't expect to be small or skinny. I would say, "After all, my mother and father at some point weighed over 300 lbs. All my aunties on my father's side of the family have at one point or another weighed over 300 lbs. My paternal grandmother as well was over 200 lbs." I even threw in my step-grandmother (no blood relationship) as an excuse since she weighed 690 lbs. at the time of her death. I won't ever forget how they had to have a graveside funeral for her because the combined weight of her and the oversized casket would have crashed through the church floor. They had to order the largest casket available and then still had to cut off both her arms so she would fit. This is one of the most disturbing and disconcerting incidents of my life. It was traumatic enough to lose her, but the manner in which it had to be done was somewhat morbid. We would eat at her house every Sunday. She was so large she had to sit and cook. But she was still an amazing cook. Every Sunday we had fried chicken, baked country ham, pot-roast with all the trimmings, deep-fried whole catfish, and fried fatback. The sides included greens, corn pudding, potato salad, macaroni and cheese, rice pudding, and an array of dessert. There was always Pepsi and sweet tea. And for added emphasis, I would say, "Please don't forget that my only uncle on my mom's side of the family has also weighed 300 lbs. on occasions." Although this was all true, it was still just a way to justify my lack of control. My hiding behind layer of fat as an excuse to cover up my real fears and disappoints in myself. Just another stopping point I had allowed the devil to infuse into my mind to keep me from EMERGING full throttle into God's intended direction for my life.

People fear you because they know that a fat person is the one thing that anyone can become. They see you as having an impaired relationship with food. Therefore, you must be inadequate in every area of your life and lacking in self-control.

I would imagine them say things like: "You don't love or value yourself ... if you did, you would take better care of yourself." "You must be lazy and undisciplined."

This kind of self-defeating thought process makes you a prime target for the devil's lies. I had lost my focus and vision from God. All my thoughts were about being overweight and what other people were thinking about my weight. There is a great danger in thinking that you know what other people are thinking. You create crazy scenarios in your mind that have no foundation and most likely will never come to pass. But regardless of the falsehood of your imagination, your body and mind still experience the same emotions, distress, and anxiety that you would if the experience was real. You ride the same emotionally-draining roller coaster of what-ifs and maybes.

Just another diversion tactic of the devil to get us to waste precious time, energy, and emotions on meaningless thoughts and deeds instead of concentrating on and doing the things necessary to be moving forward, taking new grounds, and winning souls for the Kingdom. There is not enough energy for both. At least, I couldn't find the energy for both; maybe it was carrying all that weight that was sapping up my energy. Just an afterthought.

He uses your visible faults to make you afraid to operate in your spiritual giftedness and to kill your success in other areas of your life. In your marriage, he makes you feel ashamed to be a wife to your husband. As a mother, he makes you embarrassed to be a part of your children's life because he causes you to think the other mothers will laugh at you. On your job, he makes you think that you have to tolerate mistreatments because you don't want to rock the boat and be seen as fat and bossy.

Even if you are a "bit" overweight or whatever that physical appearance aspect that you hate about yourself is, it does not disqualify you from full service for God's Kingdom.

Yes, just another lie planted in your mind as an excuse used to stop you in your tracks as you try to exercise in our ministry callings. He not only uses weight as an obstacle to block us; he uses any of our outward appearances that we may not particularly like or are uncomfortable with. And the only way to stop this vicious and consuming falsity is to stay in constant prayer, reading and studying the Scripture and positioning yourself around other woman warriors. Other strong women have, by the Grace of God, faced their excuses head-on and, in spite of them, emerged to a new level where they know who and whose they are.

Will you choose with me to focus on your future and not your physical attributes?

Do you find yourself spending too much time on your outward appearance instead of developing your inward woman?

_____

_____

_____

_____

If the answer is yes, make the commitment to spend more time in God's word this week. Write out you plan here.

_____

_____

_____

_____

Do you judge your beauty based on other women or the word of God?

_____

_____

_____

_____

The Bible is full of Scriptures that tell you how God view you as His creation. Write them here and pray them back to God

_____

_____

_____

"Fatty, fatty, two by four can't fit through the kitchen door!" How long have we been using this as an indictment to overweight people about being too large to get through a door? News flash! A 2X4 is a long slender piece of wood. I might have a problem getting through a door because of the length or height, definitely not because of its girth. Just like this, we have listened to misinformation so long we allow it to become a truth for us.

Getting Understanding:

Genesis 1:27 says, "So God created mankind in His own image, in the image of God He created them, male and female He created them."

We were "created" by God for His Glory, in His image. We are not an afterthought or accident.

"Created" infers that we were new and original, not an improvement on an old development. The image of God restored to our souls. We were made from the same earth as the beast of the fields, yet we would be different because we were flesh and spirit, heaven and earth put together. It is our souls that bear the image of God. God clothed us with authority and rules as the visible head and ruler of the world.

Housed in each of us is the divine image of God. He plants His spirit in each of us regardless of our body size, wrinkles, freckles, big feet, or whatever you deem to be your physical demon. He is not just the God of the skinny and cute. He is the God of everyone that has a heart for others and His work. Nothing is wrong with skinny and cute; I still desire them, but I have learned to fill myself with the desires of God and the needs of others.

I Samuel 16:7 states: "But the LORD said to Samuel, 'Do not consider his appearance or his height, for I have rejected him. The LORD does not look at the things people look at. People look at the outward appearance, but the LORD looks at the heart.'"

What a blessing that God not only created us but He also knows us and designed us with intent, a road map and purposeful plan of action. He knows our hearts and judges us based on that and not our outward shell.

It is interesting to notice the words in the seventh verse of this chapter, "the outward appearance"; they are translated more literally to "the eyes"; and in the twelfth verse, "a beautiful countenance" is rendered "fair of eyes." That is to say that David was not chosen for his good looks, nor was Eliab rejected because of his; they may both have had desirable eyes, but the Lord does not regard such things in His selection of people for service to Himself. Eliab was Jesse's oldest son. He is described as tall and had fair features. By law, he was the first potential King of Israel and considered for anointing by Samuel. His features resembled those Samuel had first seen in Saul, and Samuel may have considered him a fit successor to Saul. However, God told Samuel that Eliab did not have the proper heart to be King of Israel. John Milton (a legendary poet and composer of "Paradise Lost") was blind, and Thomas Carlyle (a Scottish philosopher, satirical writer, essayist, translator, historian, mathematician, and teacher during Victorian era), one of the most important social commentators of his time, although he presented many lectures during his lifetime, was not considered attractive in showy company. Paul was diminutive and half-blind, in bodily presence weak, and in speech contemptible, "but," says Chrysostom, "this man of three cubits' height became tall enough to touch the third heaven."

Look at the positive side of the statement concerning the Divine choice of a person. Since the Lord does not look at the outward appearance, what does He look at? What is meant here by the word "heart?" "The Lord seeth not as man seeth; for man looketh on the outward appearance, but the Lord looketh on the heart." "Heart" refers to the entire nature of the individual.

We can see how people look outwardly, but God can see what they are. He judges people by the heart. We often form a mistaken judgment of characters, but the Lord values only the faith, fear, and love planted in the heart, which is beyond our human discernment. David was the youngest of the sons of Jesse; his name signifies "Beloved"; he was a representation of God's beloved Son. It seemed, by our standards, that David was the least of all the sons of Jesse. But the Spirit of the Lord came upon David from that day forward. His anointing was not an empty ceremony; a Divine power went with that instituted sign; he became advanced in wisdom and courage, with all the qualifications of a prince, though nothing changed in his outward circumstances. Simply put, David was anointed as king on that day, but it would take many years before he actually took the throne. The best evidence of our being predestinated to the kingdom of glory is our being sealed with the Spirit of promise. And the promise, a promise coming from God, should be enough for us to live in the hope and expectation of the future realization of that thing for which we are waiting. Just as it took many years for David to walk in the anointing, it may take more time than you think before your true anointing is visible to others. During this time, you will have to, as they say, "trust the process." That will not change the power or effectiveness. When it is physically manifested, it will be fully operational. David had to, and you will have to, go through the preparation and training. Anointing without the proper ability to operate will be limiting and confusing.

Psalms 139:14 says, "I praise you because I am fearfully and wonderfully made, your works are wonderful, I know that full well."

Ladies, I am literally sitting here with my hands lifted in praise to God. Why does He love a wretch like me so much? I hope you will grasp the gravity of this verse the next time you start to doubt your abilities to give Him the service He deserves based on your fleshly outward characteristics. I repent right now before God.

And as the Scripture says, "I will praise thee"—God, I will not merely admire what is so great and marvelous, but I will acknowledge Thee in a public manner as wise, holy, and good: because You are entitled to honor, love, and gratitude.

"For I am fearfully and wonderfully made." Here, "fearfully" means "fearful things," things suited to produce fear or reverence. "Wonderfully made" means to distinguish, to separate. In layman's terms, "I am distinguished by fearful things" (catch this). By things in my creation which are suited to inspire awe. I am distinguished among His works by things which tend to exalt my ideas of Him and to fill my soul with reverent and devout feelings. The point is that we are "distinguished" among the works of creation, "separated" from other things in His endowments as to work in the mind a sense of awe. We were made different from inanimate objects, and from the brute creation, we were "so" made in the entire structure of His frame as to fill the mind with wonder. The more anyone contemplates his own bodily formation and becomes acquainted with the anatomy of the human frame, and the more he understands his mental organization, the more you will understand the awesomeness of God's creation of mankind.

Marvelous are thy works—fitted are they to excite wonder and admiration.

"And that my soul knoweth well," as in Hebrew, "greatly." I am fully convinced of it. I am deeply impressed by it. We can see clearly that the works of God are "wonderful," even if we can understand nothing else about them.

We must also understand the care and love with which we were formed. Instead of hating on ourselves for our outward imperfections, we must stand in awe and complete praise to the God who made us just one step lower than the angels. It would be utterly shameful to hate that which He so lovingly created.

The Spirit of God is prompting me to give you the opportunity to repent here. Take a moment, and sincerely from your heart, ask God to forgive you for hating any part of you. Give Him the praise for the marvelous creation He provided through you.

Confess any time wasted on vanity of your flesh.

_____
_____
_____
_____

Beauty is only skin deep! Well, that's what the world has to say about the matter. But as we have been learning, it is the inward beauty of the heart that God is concerned with. "Lord give us a clean heart, so we can love like you love."

I am so glad that every time the devil tries to lie to me about who I am and what I should look like, I need only to search the word of God to find truth and liberation. Yes, we should desire to look and be our best for God's glory. We can't serve as we should if our feet hurt, or we have some other preventable ailment due to our own mistreatment of our temples. So, please understand that we are not eliminated from service because of our outward appearance, but we are responsible to take great care of the physical structure that houses our spirit.

By the same token, it is a vain and futile effort to take special care of our physical appearance and neglect the inner woman. A beautiful outside is often a smokescreen to hide a black and sinful heart. People live under delusions and false pretenses to the world. Pretending to love and care when, in reality, it is just a front to cover their real intentions and deceptions. They are just acting spiritual to cover up sin. Matthew 23:28 says, "In the same manner, on the outside you appear to people as righteous but on the inside you are full of hypocrisy and wickedness." Here, Jesus is condemning the Pharisees and religious leaders for outwardly appearing saintly and holy but on the inside continuing to be full of corruption and greed. Displaying our Christianity just as a show for others is like dressing up in your best dress without having taken a bath. We are clean and pretty on the outside, but underneath, we are still filthy. It is when we are clean on the inside that our cleanliness on the outside won't be deceiving.

Take a few minutes and look up these Scriptures to be reminded that you are a precious treasure to God.

Proverbs 31:30

_____

_____

_____

_____

Ephesians 2:10

_____

_____

_____

_____

In previous readings of this Ephesians 2:10, did you catch where it says "which God prepared in advance for us to do"?

_____

_____

_____

_____

Oh My Goodness … this takes the idea that He has a plan for our lives to a whole new level. Listen, this verse is dealing with the free gift of salvation from God. He created us as His masterpiece. How dare we allow satan or others to lessen the full value of His handiwork. He values us so much that in the plan for the formation of the earth, He was preparing a way for us to be saved from our sins and to have an eternal relationship with Him. If we were to remember this and keep it at the forefront of our hearts and minds, we would not get caught up in size and body structure and any of the other visible traits that make us unique creations.

Read I Peter 3:3,4. Record the verse and your understanding here

_____

_____

_____

_____

Time in Prayer:

Oh Precious God, thank You that You have always had us on Your mind. Thank You that from the very beginning, You were making plans to provide a way of salvation for us. Help us to focus on the end price of salvation and not on our external appearance. Help us to remember that You are not looking at the outward woman but instead looking at the inward condition of our hearts and our real motives. Amen!

Your Beauty should be that of your Inner Self, the Unfading beauty of a Gentle & Quiet Spirit, which is of Great Worth in God's Sight.
1 PETER 3:3-4

CHAPTER 3:

TOO "BLACK" PHYSICAL APPEARANCE YOU WERE BORN TO THE WRONG NATIONALITY.

"Our true nationality is mankind ..."

–H.G. Wells

Much as our world is painted by a diverse assortment of cultures, languages, and ethnicities today, so it was in the world of the Bible times. Although most prejudices are associated with skin color, they also take the form of size, gender, hair texture, wealth/poverty, etc.

Some instances of prejudice mentioned in the Bible include: the Greeks considered anyone who could not speak Greek a barbarian (Galatians 3:1).

Paul was arrested by the Romans during a riot in the temple because they thought he was an Egyptian who was a troublemaker (Acts 21:38).

Often in the United States, because of territorial accent, we decide to dislike a group of people. We call southerners "rednecks" and people from the upper states "northerners."

Jesus was often identified by His accent. Although He was raised in Nazareth (Galilee), He was born in Bethlehem. His accent was Galilean, and no one considered He might actually be a Judean (John 7:41–43).

When Peter tried to deny his companionship with Jesus, his accent gave him away as a Galilean (Matthew 26:13). The list goes on and on. The Bible says in Ecclesiastes 1:9, "What has been is what will be, and what has been done is what will be done, and there is nothing new under the sun."

It really takes a low life, gutter-thinking kind of person to use something about your physical makeup against you. We all know people that have low self-esteem and low moral fiber that get great pleasure making themselves look better by pointing out and using others' seeming disadvantages against them. Holding hateful and mean opinions based on ethnic origin or some unfounded stereotype they have ascribed to. The devil loves this even more. "Girl, who is going to listen to your old, fat, black self about anything?" "Women of your race don't care what you have to say, and other races sure are not going to listen to you." I let him play this montage over and over in my mind until I started to listen. I began to feel intimidated about trying to present the Gospel to people of different races. I would shy away and feel ill-equipped to discuss the Bible with them—that's until I got into the word and started to hear what God had to say about me. How He created and loves all people. I've heard this all my church life, but for some reason, I just needed to have it reaffirmed again.

It was pointed out to me that there are people assigned to me. Assigned to me to lead to Christ, for healing, to prophesy into their life and future, and to be an example of Godly living too. And if I neglect to act or speak when God is impressing upon me, then they may not get what they are supposed to get. In some cases, their souls could be required at my hands because of my fear and disobedience. Now, that's an eye-opener. I did not want to be the cause of anyone not being in right relationship with God. I am so thankful that God sent anointed people into my life to get me on the right path and to continue to mentor me as I grow into mentoring others. An even worse thought is that if I don't do want He has assigned me or commissioned me to do, He will give it to someone else. God's work will be done, whether I do it or not.

At one point in my career, I desired to open an event facility. But because of doubt and the negative words of people close to me, I never did. I was at a girl's conference one weekend, and the daughters of one of the instructors showed up to surprise their mother. They were asked to speak briefly about their new business venture. They told how they had just opened up a premier event facility in the Richmond, VA, area. Of course, I felt some envy and regret about having not followed my dream. But the thing that floored me and caused me to grieve was when God spoke in my spirit and said, "That was your premier facility, but because of your fears and disobedience, I gave it to them." I felt it in my spirit as if I was hearing audible words. I wept with shame and disgust. People are always saying, "What is meant for you is meant for you, and no one can get what's yours." That is true if you are operating in obedience and are actively seeking and accepting what is available to you. If you are sitting around, waiting without working, or just believing that something is going to fall out of the sky in your lap, then you are sadly mistaken. No one else has to take what is yours, but if you have forfeited it with your nonacceptance or inactivity, then you have freely relinquished your right of claim. Don't let your unfounded fears and excuse rob you of your blessings. God still has great blessings for me and even an event facility if I still desire that. My point is, as they say, "One monkey don't stop no show." Just because you fail to act or move when God calls doesn't mean His work will not go on or move forward. You may lose out … but the work of God will continue on. Your "No" only hinders your forward movement; God's plan will always be accomplished.

Ethnic origin has long been a means of disqualifying us as being able to do many things throughout the years. Or hasn't it? If we are a people trusting and believing in God and that He is in control of us and our destiny, can we really use this as an excuse for not succeeding? God created us all. He created us each with limitless opportunity and possibility. Our current state is a result of our choices and decisions. Therefore, I choose God; I choose a future full of hope and promises, and I choose to "emerge victorious."

When I was 7 years old, we moved to a small community called "Hells Bend." It was a small all-white community except for two other families that were bi-racial. We played together all summer the year we moved. We stayed out all day long. The only rule our parents had was to be home before dark. So, we wandered all over the neighborhood to each other's homes, just having good old childhood fun. I honestly did not realize that there was different because I was black until the first day of school. It started the moment we stepped on the bus. The name-calling, hair pulling, and constant racial jokes. I was totally confused because we had played together all summer without any of this foolishness. Did I mention that this was the first year of intergraded schools in Campbell County, VA? It was a living nightmare every day. The really strange thing was that when we would get home each evening, we would all play together again as if the events of the school day had not happened. Thinking back on this, I get tickled because it reminds me of the cartoon *Don't Give Up The Sheep* in which Ralph Wolf and Sam Sheepdog spend all day with Sam, trying to protect the sheep from Ralph, and Ralph is determined by any means necessary to get a sheep for his dinner. They would fight and try to destroy each other by dropping rocks on each other, running over each other, and shooting each other with rockets and bow and arrows. Then at lunchtime, they would clock out, have lunch together under the tree, chatting and making nice. The alarm would sound, announcing the end of lunch. The scene would immediately pan back to the exact moment they left off. It would be in the middle of a rock dropping or a bombing going off. At 5 o'clock, they both would clock out and go have drinks together. Then the next morning at 6 AM, the whole scenario starts all over again. It is seriously crazy the things that we allow, accept, and actively participates in that moves us no closer to the end result we are seeking. We futilely repeat the same things over and over with the same outcome. We, with our eyes wide open, keep walking into the same day; same unhelpful, uncaring, selfish people. We would rather keep failing at the same thing than to be courageous enough to step into the unknown and find our destiny and purpose. We run here and there, chasing people and the dream, when all we have to do is get lined up with God. He is speaking to each of us. We don't even have to waste energy pondering and figuring.

It has been said many times that "the devil doesn't have any new tricks, just new faces." For example, in Genesis 27:46, Rebekah screams her frustration with Esau's wives because of their ethnic background. She was not moved or upset that he had more than one wife. "I am disgusted with living because of these Hittite women," she tells Isaac. "If Jacob takes a wife from among the women of this land, from the Hittite women like these, my life will not be worth living." This comment is loaded with racial connotations. The devil loves to use our wonderful differences against us. These should be the thing that causes us to communicate, share, and learn about each other.

Just as he divided the women of the Bible because they didn't all look just alike, he is doing the very same thing today. We should be mature enough as women of God to recognize those same old tactics and not fall prey to them. So many times, we see the setup as it unfolds before our eyes, yet we fall in that same hole over and over.

I.

I walk down the street.
There is a deep hole in the sidewalk.
I fall in.
I am lost.
I am hopeless.
It isn't my fault.
It takes forever to find a way out.

II.

I walk down the same street.
There is a deep hole in the sidewalk.
I pretend I don't see it.
I fall in again.
I can't believe I'm in the same place.
But it isn't my fault.
It still takes a long time to get out.

III.

I walk down the same street.
There is a deep hole in the sidewalk.
I see it there.
I still fall in … it's a habit.
My eyes are open; I know where I am.
It is my fault.
I get out immediately.

IV

I walk down the same street.
There is a deep hole in the sidewalk.
I walk around it

V

I walk down another street.

By Portia Nelson

This poem is so cute and catchy, but what a profound message hidden between the lines. To do better, you must recognize you need to do better and then "Just get 'er done."

An essential component of everyone's life should be a circle of friends or maybe that one special friend that will call you out when you have gotten off track. It is so important to have that tribe of women that you can trust to speak the absolute truth to you, no matter how much it hurts or offends. We need people that will make you look in the mirror and talk to yourself about yourself. It is most often true that we don't see our dysfunctions until they are lovingly pointed out to us. But once we have that talk with ourselves, we can turn this thing around and begin "breaking the mold" and making the steps toward a fresh start with Christ at the center of every area of our lives.

Getting Understanding

Galatian 3:28 states, "There is neither Jew nor Greek, there is neither slave nor free, there is no male and female for you are all one in Christ Jesus."

The primitive church consisted of both Jew and Greek. God made no difference between them. He died for both. When the middle wall of partition was torn down, the Gospel was equally available to both. And both were equally as sinful; belief in Christ gave them the same opportunity to benefit from the gospel and share in the blessings of His grace.

So it is with us today. God is no respecter of national origin. He offers His salvation and grace freely to all who call on His name to be saved.

As women of the faith, we cannot afford to be ill-informed or just plain old ignorant because we don't have the luxury of wasting time; Jesus is soon to come back. God is not using our skin color and ethnic background to deem us unsuitable for service. He has called all people to salvation, and thus, all people must be represented as we shout the battle cry. Matthew 28:14 (NIV) says, "Therefore go and make disciples of all nations, baptizing them in the name of the Father and of the Son and of the Holy Spirit." Go ye therefore ... into all the world. Previously, this authority and power belonged to Judea only ... but now it was extended to all nations of the world. That includes every ethnic background.

Society and the devil want to silence the voice of God from going forth by making false claims against us because of our cultural differences. God is concerned with the state of our hearts and the accuracy of the message. Foolishly, man is the one who is looking at our outward house based on our national origin.

In Luke 19:40, God declares, "... if they keep quiet the stones will cry out." So, are we supposed to believe that He will make the rocks cry out, but He will not use a woman of color or other nationality?" That is absurd.

There is a great host of ethnic presences recorded in the Bible. The Bible does not directly say black or African;

however, it does use Ethiopians, Cushites, Egyptians, Hebrews, and other ethnic tribal terms. Ethiopia is referenced more than 45 times, and Africa is mentioned more than any other landmass in the Bible. The "middle east," including the Holy Land, was connected to Africa until 1959 when the Suez Canal was completed and has been referred to as North Africa for the majority of history.

Many of the Hebrew patriarchs married or had children with women of African tribes. Abraham had children with Hagar and Keturah, both from Africa (Hamitic) tribes. Moses married Zipporah, who was Ethiopian. Jacob had children with two handmaidens from African tribes, and these children (Dan, Naphtali, Gad, and Asher) became the patriarchs of two tribes of Israel.

Black people and all other ethnicities have played a central role in God's plan for humanity and were not an afterthought of our great creator.

"And He made from one man every nation of mankind to live on the face of the earth, having determined allotted periods and the boundaries of their dwelling place, that they should seek God, in the hope that they might feel their way toward Him and find Him. Yet He is actually not far from each of us" (Acts 17:26–27).

Paul settles the matter quite simply here with this text. God made us all from one man, one bloodline—Adam. All the families of mankind are products of one original origin. No matter how different our complexion, body features, national language, we are derived from a common lineage.

"Blood" is often used to denote "race, stock, kindred." This text affirms that all the entire human family is descended from one source. Even after the flood, the earth was repopulated through one seed, that of Noah.

Paul also wanted them to understand that we are all considered brethren and that although he was a Jew, he was not enslaved to any narrow notion or prejudices in regard to other people. No one nation or individual can claim any superiority over another in virtue of birth or blood. We are all equal in this regard; the entire human family, regardless of our outward differences of customs and laws, are to be considered and treated as brethren.

My Sister, God created you beautiful and totally capable, no matter your national background. He did not make any of us to be the dirt underneath another human being's feet. We have equal value and equal opportunities through the freedom Christ's dying on the cross created. Don't make His sacrifice trivial by not accepting what He gave His life for you to be able to enjoy.

I love how everything God does has order and purpose. There are no random or accidental occurrences with God. "Having determined allotted periods and the boundaries of their dwelling place …" Wow moment for me. God had, in His plans, fixed the times when each country should be settled, rise, prosper, and even fall. The different continents and islands were not established by chance but by the wise rule of God and in perfect accordance with His arrangement and design. EMERGING from our ethnic, racial, and diversity prejudices takes intentional actions on all of our parts.

Read Genesis 11:1–9

What fresh or different view point do you have about this verse?

_____

_____

_____

_____

Can you see how the Old Testament connects with future events and prophesy?

_____

_____

_____

_____

Do you get a clearer picture of God's order and planning for our lives?

_____

_____

_____

_____

If (since) (because) God was so meticulous in creating the boundaries of civilization, creating the order by which the earth would exist, and defining the rules by which everything would co-exist because of its co-dependency one upon the other, do you not think that He would take even greater care to ensure that we have all that is necessary to function within that domain? And that we, too, would be dependent one upon the other for spiritual and natural survival? God makes all things to work in harmony and unison. No one person possesses everything they need to function. We are created to need each other. In light of that, why would God then design a world that divides us by skin color or nationality? We are divided because of our selfish, prideful sin nature.

Look up, read, and record each of the below Scriptures. How does each shed light on the design of God for oneness in the faith?

Colossians 3:11

_____
_____
_____
_____

Ezekiel 47:22

_____
_____
_____
_____

We are all created with Kingdom purpose and a desire for something better than we have in this body of flesh. This desire is lost as we grow and become affected by our environment, family, friends, and experiences. Satan uses these same situations to study us and to formulate his plan to derail us. God has a plan for our success and prosperity; satan has a plan for our destruction and failure. What is your plan of action? You get to choose which plan you will accept and pursue.

The Bible says in Romans 2:11, "God does not show favoritism." That includes race or national origin. Make a choice with me to not allow satan to use the beautiful person God assigned you to be against you. Instead, enjoy being a daughter of God with the full benefits of your Father.

Revelation 7:9–10: "After this I looked, and behold, a great multitude that no one could number, from every nation, from all tribes and peoples and languages, standing before the throne and before the Lamb, clothed in white robes, with palm branches in their hands, and crying out with a loud voice, "Salvation belongs to our God who sits on the throne and to the Lamb!

Wow, wow, wow, "a great multitude from every nation, from all tribes and people and languages." Like they say, "all" means "all." Same here. "Every" means "every." Every race and national origin will be represented on this great day. There are no exceptions, exclusion, or exemptions associated with skin tone or place of birth in the verse. The only stipulation is that you have lived a life in obedience to the ordinance and commands of God's Holy word. God loves each of us and has placed redeeming power in us all.

Why would a God that loves you so much that He has included you in reigning with Him in Heaven eliminate you from a lifetime of service to Him through the giftedness HE has placed within you? It seems totally ridiculous when you say it out loud, doesn't it? You are good enough to be saved and to live with Him forever but not good enough to lead others or minister to His people. Sometimes the devil's attempts are so weak and lame that we should be embarrassed to even acknowledge that we gave the slightest bit of thought to them.

As mature women of the Most High God, we know that we have power and dominion over the devil and our flesh. As aged, mature, Christian women emerging into our spiritual destinies, we must understand that ethnic prejudice is reprehensible. Columnist, Jack White, wrote, "the most insidious racism is among those who don't think they harbor any. Those of us who leave our ethnic stereotypes unexamined will surely carry them forever, even pass them on to others."

Time in Prayer:

Dear God, thank You for Your unconditional love for all mankind. We praise You because You are not a respecter of persons. Help me to take my rightful place as Your child. Help me to stand boldly and to declare Your word and wisdom to all flesh and nations. Amen.

Nationalities Mentioned in the Bible

Arabians, Assyrians, Babylonians, Cretes, Cyprus, Edomites, Egyptians, Ethiopians, French, Magog/Gogs, Greeks, Indians, Iranians, Israelites, Italians, Judeans, Lebanon,

Libyans, Macedonians, Malts, Spanish, Sudanese, Syrians, Turkish

20 of the Most Influential Women in History … Paul Riner

(These brilliant, gifted women come from all nationalities)

1. <u>Princess Diana</u> (1961–1997). Princess of Wales, married to Prince Charles. Later divorced. Known for her humanitarian and charity work.

2. <u>Indira Gandhi</u> (1917–1984). Third Prime Minister of India, 1966–1977 and 1980–1984. Influential in shaping post-war Indian constitution and society.

3. <u>Queen Victoria</u> (1819–1901). Queen of Great Britain during the nineteenth century. Oversaw dramatic rise in prominence of Great Britain and her Empire.

4. <u>Madonna</u> (1958–). American singer and songwriter. Often noted for her controversial lyrics and activities. Best-selling female artist of all time.

5. <u>Mary Magdalene</u> (4 BCE–40 CE). A devotee of Jesus Christ. Present at Christ's crucifixion and the first person to see Jesus after His resurrection.

6. <u>Benazir Bhutto</u> (1953–2007). Prime Minister of Pakistan. The first woman to lead a Muslim state.

7. <u>Jacqueline Kennedy Onassis</u> (1929–1994). Wife of John F. Kennedy. Cultural and fashion icon of the 1960s.

8. <u>Cleopatra</u> (69 BCE–30 BCE). Last Pharaoh of ancient

Egypt. Had relationship with Roman rulers Julius Caesar and Mark Anthony.

9. Joan of Arc (1412–1431). Young girl who inspired French to revolt against British rule. Burnt at the stake for witchcraft.

10. Marilyn Monroe (1926–1962). Actress, model, and icon of post-war America.

11. Mother Teresa (1910–1997). Nun and charity worker. Mother Teresa dedicated her life to serving the poor and disadvantaged.

12. Anne Frank (1929–1945). Jewish diarist who documented her life in hiding in an Amsterdam attic during the Nazi occupation. Died in Belsen concentration camp.

13. Audrey Hepburn (1929–1993). Actress. Voted greatest female screen legend of all time. Fashion icon and humanitarian who worked for UNICEF.

14. Oprah Winfrey (1954–) Chat show host and icon of American women. Winfrey's chat show and book club are very influential.

15. Billie Jean King (1943–). Tennis player and advocate for equality between men and women.

16. Eleanor of Aquitaine (1122–1204). Queen of France and one of the wealthiest and most powerful women of the Middle Ages.

17. Hilary Clinton (1947–). US Secretary of State 2009–2013. First lady during Bill Clinton's presidency and Democratic

candidate for President in 2008 and 2016.

18. Brigitte Bardot (1934–). French actress, dancer, singer, and animal rights activist.

19. Eleanor Roosevelt (1884–1962). American wife of F.D. Roosevelt and human rights campaigner.

20. Coco Chanel (1883–1971). Fashion designer and founder of fashion label Chanel. Influential in the 1920s for setting new fashion trends which broke with previous styles.

CHAPTER 4:

TOO "FEMALE" GENDER BIAS

"Women, like good little children, should be seen and not heard."

—Unknown

I hope the fathers and mothers of little girls will look at them and say 'Yes, women can.'"

—Dilma Rousseff

My first memories of church are my childhood days at the Miracle Revival Holiness Church in my local community of Long Island, VA. My uncle Eugene was the senior pastor, and my aunt Corrine was the associate pastor. Uncle Eugene is my mom's only brother. It was just the two of them. Their mother died giving birth to my mother, and then their father passed when my mother was only five years old. They were then raised by an aunt.

Besides being the associate pastor, my aunt was loved and envied because she made a mean meatloaf. She had this special glaze she made to go on top and her secret ingredient. When we had church suppers, everyone would come to her table, asking for that, as my granddaughter Christiana says, "smack-arduous" meatloaf. She explained to me that smack-arduous meant it was so good it made you want to smack someone.

So, it baffles me that since having grown up with women in leadership in the church all my childhood, as an adult I begin to believe that women should be almost invisible as it relates to the leadership and teaching of God's people.

I've tried to pinpoint that moment in time when my thought processes changed and to also lay finger on the incident that re-forged my opinion.

Later, my mother, sisters, one of my brothers, and I attended Grace Baptist Church. The pastor there married my husband and I. I meet Leon when I was twelve years old on the school bus. For some unknown reason, they changed the bus route that year, and instead of going to the west end of Tabor Road, it took a right and went to the east end. Little did I know that that small shift in direction would change my life forever. Because at the east end of the route was this fine, brown, big-lipped young man named Leon Hubbard. He stepped onto the school bus wearing pink denim jeans and a multi-colored shirt he had unbuttoned to reveal his chest. He also had on 4-inch platform shoes. And did I mention he was bow-legged and was sporting the biggest afro I had ever seen on a man? He sat beside me. I stopped breathing. We didn't talk that day, but he asked me to marry him the second day, and the rest is history. Here we are, 39 years later, and I love him more than I even understood was possible way back then. We talked on the bus and wrote letters over the summer for several years. Then I was finally sixteen, and we could go out.

After getting married, I moved my membership to the St. Luke Baptist Church because of my belief that a husband and wife should attend the same church and be under the same doctrine of teaching. In 1995, we moved to the Hills Creek Baptist Church. We felt led by God to move there since it was in the neighborhood in which we lived. We both felt that our time, talent, and tithe should be invested in our own surrounding with the people that had the same vested interest in the success of the community as we did.

I've spent considerable time pondering this shift in my thinking. I recall being taught that women were not to have any roles of leadership, teaching men, or preaching. I begin to fade into the background and to do a lot of behind-the-scene things. I directed the youth choir, taught women's Sunday School, acted as the Sunday School secretary, and worked a little with the financial recording. However, every so often I would get this desire to do more or that there is greater in me. I would tell my husband, "I don't know what God has for me to do, but I feel like He's calling me out to lead." My husband, Leon, was just as dogmatic about the position of women, so I would just go back to business as usual and be happy for a period of time. But still, every so often, that uneasiness and unfulfillment would rise up in me again.

My daughter, Tiffany, and I would have these conversations about my desires. I would ask her how I was supposed to be obedient to the call God had on my life and to also be submitted to a husband that does not believe in what I say God is calling me to do. I spent a lot of time frustrated and bitter because I could not understand why God would call me out and then give me a pastor and husband that do not believe that I could even be called. How do you emerge, come into your destiny, or break from behind the scenes when you are battling your own uncertainty and that of every man of influence and impact to your personal beliefs around you?

I would study the Scriptures that centered around women's roles in the church. If I was studying the pros, it seemed right on point, and the Scripture supported what I was reading. Then if I was studying the cons, same thing; the scriptural references used would totally support the writer's point of view. I was so crazy confused that I just stopped trying to figure it out.

I prayed, fasted, and talked to other leaders. I was a mess. I was living that old adage that says, "You can use the Scripture to support most any opinion you have if you take it out of context." All I knew was that that impression in my spirit that I should be ministering and leading would not die.

When I look back at my life and work history, everywhere I have worked or volunteered, they would always put me in charge. They didn't know me, but they would see something in me that says, "She can lead this group to success." And 99% of the time, I did. During those times, I never considered myself as a leader. I even resented having to always be the person responsible for ensuring that everyone did what they were supposed to and having the obligation and weight of the success or failure fall on my shoulders.

All of the elements were there. I had not recognized them for what they meant. My skills and abilities just needed to be honed and re-directed. My guess would be that you have or are experiencing the same type of interactions in your daily life. You, too, have patterns of behavior or traits that just keep reappearing, yet you have not taken the time to define why or what it means in your search for your calling.

I had my hands in every women's ministry and behind-the-scene function of the church; financial secretary, chairperson of the Deaconess, head of the Children's Church Department, working on the finance committee, and on every other yearly committee that was formed. I was exhausted, but I got it done and done well. I did not understand the art of a good "No." The statement most often was, "Barbara will get it done." The leader and perfectionist in me would not lay down and just die, even though I had sold my destiny to the lying voice of the devil and every man that told me to shut up, be quiet, and sit down. "Woman should be seen and not heard," right?

It is a terrible, crippling, and spiritually draining position to be in when you allow false doctrine and misuse of the Scripture to determine your obedience to God and effectiveness in your kingdom work. I had to come to the point that I realized that obedience is more important than appearance to man. That nagging reminder showed up again to remind me that one day I was going to die and have to stand "ALONE" before God with no reasonable explanation for my excuses. Or I may end up as this old woman, alone and regretful. Once again, the real "scared straight" moment. "Fear not them that kill the body, but are not able to kill the soul; but rather fear Him who is able to destroy both the soul and body in hell" (Matthew 10:28).

While at the lowest and most defeated point of my life, my daughter came to me with a suggestion. She had taken a leadership class under Pastor Nicole Bonds of the Life Church. She was so excited and empowered. She said she thought I would really benefit from taking the class. Man, I had so many reservations and apprehensions I was getting sick at the stomach. My head was spinning, and my heart was torn. She was everything I was taught a woman couldn't be. She was female, a pastor, an apostle, and divorced. Oh my goodness … I was never going to be a part of this.

I never have a problem sleeping; all I need is to be still for about a minute, and I can go to sleep. Not the narcolepsy kind of sleep at anytime, anywhere, even if you didn't want to sleep. But instead, once I'm done and in bed, I'm out totally—as soon as my head hits the pillow. But this thing was keeping me up at night and invading my every thought during the day. So, I signed up for the next session of the class (LeadU, Kingdom Leaders) and made my appointment for my first ever one-on-one consultation. I went in with all my prejudices and with my shield up. Within 10 minutes, I was in love with this woman of God. She had the most comforting and motherly spirit ever, although she is almost

15 years my junior. Over the course of a year, we talked about what I believed. I even told her that she was nothing that I believed in; she didn't even blink. She unpacked the Scriptures with me, told me things about me that only God could have told her because He was the only one that knew them, prophesied over my life, and empowered me to go forth and lead. Had I listened to the voice in my head telling me to disregard her based on my misguided perception of what a woman of God should look like, I would have missed out on a beautiful life-long new relationship with an anointed-giving vessel of God and the EMERGING transformation that forged out of her loving and Bible-based teachings to dis-spell my faulty thinking.

After going through this class, I finally had the nerve and confidence to tell Leon that I had been called by God to minister and lead an army of women to do battle for the kingdom of God. He did not like it one bit. He said he thought we had agreed that woman could not hold authority over men in the church. I explained that I was not called to pastor; I was called to ministry and that I would be preaching my initial sermon on December 3, 2017, at the Life Church in Lynchburg, VA, under Apostle Nicole Bonds, founder of Exousia Global Fellowship. We spent many days debating and trying to make sense of this. Every time I thought he was at a place of understanding, he would come back with something else to try to discourage me or change my mind. I pressed on; I couldn't say no to God again … I was afraid for me and him.

Tiffany, two other ladies from the class, and I would be doing a four-way sermon on the seasons of ministry using the four seasons of nature. I would be the only one licensed, even though we all had to speak. The others did not feel they had been called to pulpit ministry, although they were each called to other areas of the ministry. I chose "fall" because that is where I felt I was in life. So, in a crowd of family, friends, and church family, I, a woman, stood and preached the message of Jesus Christ and received my official license to preach. It was a two-day weekend event. Saturday was our graduation and celebration dinner event, and then we would all preach or teach on Sunday.

At graduation, we were all required to make a speech about what we had gained from the program and the plans we had for using the knowledge we had received. While I sat and waited for my turn to speak, I kept trying to form some kind of outline for what I would say. I had something prepared, but as I sat there, it wasn't feeling like what God wanted me to say. To those around me, I probably appeared nervous about having to speak, but that was not it. I was at war in my heart and head, trying to make all of this make some kind of sense to me. It was like the commercial where you see the devil sitting on one shoulder and an angel sitting on the other of someone trying to make a decision. They are both talking at the same time, pleading their case in the ear of the victim. The victim is in complete turmoil, battling with himself.

When it came time for me to speak, I thanked Pastor Nicole and talked about my love for her and her tolerance of my narrow-mindedness. I was speaking with my mouth while this internal turmoil continued to take place in my heart and spirit. I kept thinking, *I can't start this new phase of my relationship with God living behind this fake relationship with Leon. I know he loves me.* And because of the battle I had fought in my own struggle to let go of my old beliefs, I understood how hard it was for him to do the same. We are products of our background, the things we have been taught, the traditions of our family, and the flavor of the church we attend. Here was this 59-year-old man who's used to things just like they were, and all of a sudden, the woman he loves is rocking their world with all this new stuff. He didn't want new stuff; everything was fine just as it was in his viewpoint. He was trying to go alone because he loved me, and he could see the turmoil inside me. He could also see the difference in me since I started standing for what I believed and had submitted to God's call. He could see the calmness, softer words, and all the time I was spending in prayer and Bible study. He witnessed the fruits of my "Yes." I understood that it had taken me 55 years to stop running and that I had pretty much changed overnight, so I was going to have to give him some time to process it all and to make the adjustment. I understood all of that, but at this moment in time, "what's love got to do with it" when I'm dying on the inside, trying to please this man that I loved to "death" and the God of creation who loves me to "life"? My mind said, "Wait one minute. I'm called to give life to the people of God, and I'm dying." The two and the two here are not equaling four. I can't move forward until we settle this thing once and for all. You are either all in or all out; there is no middle ground. You can't support what you don't believe in. No amount of so-called love can cover that. I was not going to live a lie, and I definitely was not going to live in a daily war zone battling over our differences in beliefs in how we saw women's roles in the church. His mind and heart needed to be in agreement. He couldn't just support and believe in me and not believe in every other woman. It just doesn't work that way.

In the middle of this internal battle, the battle that was not matching the words I was speaking, I looked at Leon, and I began to cry. I cried because I felt like his being there to "support me" was a lie. A lie because I knew how he felt; he had told me he did not believe in what I was doing. Before I could think about what I was saying, I began to tell him I was about to speak the truth about us being there. I apologized to him if this would cause him any embarrassment, but it had to be said so someone else there could be set free, healed, and step up to emerge into their call also. He began to shake and cry also because he knew what I was about to confront. I told him that he was forcing me to make a decision, a decision that did not have to be made. It would be his decision and not mine. I felt like I had to choose him or God while knowing that I could have both. He was forcing me to choose between the love of my life and the God that had lovingly given me a new life. But if he made me choose them, I would have to choose God. I felt the release of the internal torture I had been enduring for months. When I finished and look up, the whole room was crying with us. I walked off stage and into his crying arms, not sure what that meant for us but ready to accept whatever the repercussion would be.

During lunch, several ladies told me that they were in the same battle at home. They were struggling with how to function in their calling while trying to maintain a marital relationship with a spouse that does not believe a woman should preach or lead in the church. I explained that I didn't have an answer yet either. But with much prayer, fasting, hearing from God through His word, He would provide us with everything we would need; His assurance, His love, and His revelation.

All of the other lies of the devil that I allowed to become my excuse, "too old, too, too fat, too black" had been true stopping points that hindered my journey to preach the gospel of Christ. But this one right here, "too female," was the one that almost ended it all. It was a true battle of my soul and mind. I seriously grappled and wrestled with my beliefs and what my heart was telling me. For the first time in my life, I couldn't eat or swallow. It literally took my breath away to think about the possible outcome of this dilemma. In my mind, I just couldn't see how this was going to end well. Lose my marriage or lose my calling. I have several dear sisters that lost their marriage because their spouse could not make the adjustment.

I've told you about my strained journey and the resolution I came to. I stand by that decision and feel that I have been released or freed since making it. To me, the evidence of the right choice is the fruit that is produced afterward. The fruit has been plentiful and rich. I've seen great changes in myself, my spouse, and relationship with God. I have experienced spiritual growth and never been more confident in my current position.

In this section, I just want to present the scriptural reference to females in leadership positions in the church and let you earnestly partition God for yourself on the direction He wants you to seek for your life. This is a very controversial issue, and you should find full conviction from God for yourself. Marriage, remarriage, divorce, tithing, and baptism are all issues that are often debated. One denomination teaches this, and another teaches that, and they both use the same scripture to support or refute the same never-ending discussion. The word of God teaches us in 2 Timothy 2:15, "Study to show yourself approved unto God, a workman that needeth not to be ashamed, rightly dividing the word of truth." It also says in Romans 14:24, "But if you have doubts whether or not you should eat something, you are sinning if you go ahead and do it. For you are not following your conviction. If you do anything you believe is not right, you are sinning." So, maybe if nothing else, this section will make you get out your Bible, pen, and paper and do some good old-fashioned Bible study.

The principles and techniques in this book not only apply to EMERGING into the woman of God you are called to be; it is also very practical and useful practices for your daily living, in your business or work life, or anytime you need to sure up your confidence or weigh out a decision.

Getting Understanding:

Judges 4:4-5 – "Now Deborah, a prophet, the wife of Lappidoth, was leading Israel at that time. 5. She held court under the Palm of Deborah between Ramah and Bethel in the hill country of Ephraim, and the Israelites went up to her to have their disputes decided."

Bible Commentary: The Bible records several women who held national leadership positions. Obviously, she was the best person for the job, and God chose her to lead Israel. God can and does chose anyone to lead His people, young, old, male, or female. Deborah was an exceptional woman and leader.

The Matthew Henry Commentary says that Deborah was a prophetess, one instructed in Divine knowledge by the inspiration of the Spirit of God. She judged Israel as God's mouth to them, correcting abuses and redressing grievances. By God's direction, she ordered Barak to raise an army and engage Jabin's forces. Barak insisted much upon her presence. Deborah promised to go with him. She would not send him where she would not go herself. Those who in God's name call others to their duty should be ready to assist them in it. Barak values the satisfaction of his mind and the good success of his enterprise more than mere honor.

2 Kings 22:8–20: "[8.] And Hilkiah the high priest said unto Shaphan the scribe, I have found the book of the law in the house of the Lord. And Hilkiah gave the book to Shaphan, and he read it. [9.] And Shaphan the scribe came to the king, and brought the king word again, and said, Thy servants have gathered the money that was found in the house, and have delivered it into the hand of them that do the work, that have the oversight of the house of the Lord. [10.] And Shaphan the scribe shewed the king, saying, Hilkiah the priest hath delivered me a book. And Shaphan read it before the king. [11.] And it came to pass, when the king had heard the words of the book of the law, that he rent his clothes. [12.] And the king commanded Hilkiah the priest, and Ahikam the son of Shaphan, and Achbor the son of Michaiah, and Shaphan the scribe, and Asahiah a servant of the king's, saying, [13.] Go ye, enquire of the Lord for me, and for the people, and for all Judah, concerning the words of this book that is found: for great is the wrath of the Lord that is kindled against us, because our fathers have not hearkened unto the words of this book, to do according unto all that which is written concerning us. [14.] So Hilkiah the priest, and Ahikam, and Achbor, and Shaphan, and Asahiah, went unto **Huldah the prophetess, the wife of Shallum the son of Tikvah, the son of Harhas, keeper of the wardrobe; (now she dwelt in Jerusalem in the college;) and they communed with her.** [15.] And she said unto them, Thus saith the Lord God of Israel, Tell the man that sent you to me, [16.] Thus saith the Lord, Behold, I will bring evil upon this place, and upon the inhabitants thereof, even all the words of the book which the king of Judah hath read: [17.] Because they have forsaken me, and have burned incense unto other gods, that they might provoke me to anger with all the works of their hands; therefore my wrath shall be kindled against this place, and shall not be quenched. [18.] But to the king of Judah which sent you to enquire of the Lord, thus shall ye say to him,

Thus saith the Lord God of Israel, As touching the words which thou hast heard; [19.] Because thine heart was tender, and thou hast humbled thyself before the Lord, when thou heardest what I spake against this place, and against the inhabitants thereof, that they should become a desolation and a curse, and hast rent thy clothes, and wept before me; I also have heard thee, saith the Lord. [20.] Behold therefore, I will gather thee unto thy fathers, and thou shalt be gathered into thy grave in peace; and thine eyes shall not see all the evil which I will bring upon this place. And they brought the king word again."

Bible Commentary: Verse 14 - Huldah was a prophetess, so were Miriam (Exodus 15:20) and Deborah (Judges 4:4). God freely selects his servants to carry out His will. He chooses the rich or poor, man or woman, king or slave (Joel 2:28–40). Huldah was obviously highly regarded by the people of her time.

<u>Proverbs 31:26</u> – "She openeth her mouth with wisdom; and in her tongue [is] the law of kindness."

Bible Commentary: She is an example of a meek and quiet spirit. She manages her household well, with economy and discretion. She instructs her household in practical religion and industry and is an excellent example of godliness. She is business-minded and makes provision for her husband, family, and the future.

<u>Joel 2:28-32</u> – "[28.] Then afterward I will pour out my spirit on all flesh; your sons and your daughters shall prophesy,

your old men shall dream dreams, and your young men shall see visions. ²⁹· Even on the male and female slaves, in those days, I will pour out my spirit. ³⁰· I will show portents in the heavens and on the earth, blood and fire and columns of smoke. ³¹· The sun shall be turned to darkness, and the moon to blood, before the great and terrible day of the Lord comes. ³²· Then everyone who calls on the name of the Lord shall be saved; for in Mount Zion and in Jerusalem there shall be those who escape, as the Lord has said, and among the survivors shall be those whom the Lord calls."

Bible Commentary: This same verse is quoted in Acts 2:16-21 by Peter. This outpouring occurred during Pentecost. In the past, God's Spirit appeared to only be available to kings, prophets, and judges. Here, Joel envisions a time when all believers would have access to the Spirit. Ezekiel 39:28 29 also speaks of this outpouring of the Spirit. God's Spirit is available NOW to everyone who calls on the Lord.

<u>Acts 2:17</u>, 18 – "And it shall come to pass in the last days, saith God, I will pour out of my Spirit upon all flesh: and your sons and your daughters shall prophesy, and your young men shall see visions, and your old men shall dream. dreams: ¹⁸· And on my servants and on my handmaidens I will pour out in those days of my Spirit; and they shall prophesy."

Bible Commentary: This is once again the prediction of Joel's prophecy being fulfilled in the "last days." Here, "poured out" literally means to gush out, to spill freely, or pour out abundantly. This spirit was given not to supersede the Scripture but instead to enable us to understand and apply the Scripture. It would fall on all flesh; not just Jews but upon the Gentiles as well. The Spirit in them would be the Spirit of prophecy. They would be empowered to foretell the future and preach the gospel. This power would be granted without differentiation of sex (sons ... daughters shall prophesy), without partiality based on age (young men shall see vision ... old men). They would receive divine revelation to be relayed to the church (servants and handmaids). Men and women without distinctions of outward conditions, even the servants and handmaids, shall receive the Spirit of prophecy.

Acts 18:26 – "And he began to speak boldly in the synagogue: whom when Aquila and Priscilla had heard, they took him unto [them], and expounded unto him the way of God more perfectly."

Bible Commentary: In this age when the focus is mostly on what occurs between husbands and wives, Aquila and Priscilla are an illustration of what can evolve through husbands and wives. Their effectiveness speaks of their relationship with God and each other. Couples should make the most of their combined lives by complementing each other and capitalizing on each other's strengths to form an effective team. They are never mentioned separately in the Bible. Not in their marriage or ministry.

Acts 21:9 – "And the same man had four daughters, virgins, which did prophesy."

Bible Commentary: Obviously the gift of prophecy was given to both men and women. Women actively participated in God's work (Acts 2:17, Philippians 4:3). Again, other women who prophesied include Miriam (Exodus 15:20), Deborah (Judges 4:4), Huldah (2 Kings 22:14), Noadiah (Nehemiah 6:14), Isaiah's wife (Isaiah 8:3), and Anna (Luke 2:36–38).

This Commentator also lists 9 Reasons for Women Preaching:

1. In the Gospels, we read of several women messengers who proclaimed the "good news" (Mat. 28:1–10, Lk. 24:9–11, Jn. 4:28–30; 20:16–18).
2. In Acts 2:14–21, Joel 2:28–31, God predicts and promised that He Himself would pour His Spirit upon women, and they would prophesy. To prophesy means to "speak to men to edification, exhortation, and comfort" (I Corn. 14:3). "He that prophesied edifieth the church" (I Corn. 14:4). Prophesying is for the church and general public (Corn. 12:1–31; 14:1-6; 12:24–26, 29–33).
3. In Acts 21:8–9, it is clear that Philip's four daughters were prophetesses, i.e., they were evangelists like their father. This is in perfect accord with Joel 2:28–29 which was fulfilled in the early church (Acts 2:16) and with Acts 2:17–18 which will be fulfilled in the last days.
4. In Romans 16, we have record of a number of women servants of the Lord in various churches. Phebe (v. 1–2). Priscilla (v. 3–5), Mary, Tryphena, Tryphosa, Persis, and Julia (v. 6–15) are mentioned as laborers in the Lord.

5. In Phil. 4:2, Euodias and Syntyche are mentioned as being leaders of the church at Philippi.
6. Corinthian women prophesied and prayed in the church (I Corn. 11:4–5), so the Scripture in I Corn. 14:34–35 that is used to condemn women preachers does not refer to preaching but to disturbances in the church services—asking or talking out to their husbands in the church, as stated in I Corn. 14:35. Even so with I Tim. 2:11–15, Paul is not condemning women preaching as long as they keep their place and do not "usurp" authority over the man. Both men and women at Corinth were permitted to pray and prophesy but were regulated by fixed laws in doing so (I Corn. 14:24–32).
7. In I Corn. 12, Paul compares the church to a human body and mentions 9 gifts of the Spirit, including the gift of prophecy for all the members of the body of Christ, men and women.
8. Women were used of God in O.T. days as prophetess (Ex 15:20, Judg. 4:4; 2 Kings 22:14, 2 Chron. 34:22; Neh. 6:14; Isa. 8:3, Lk. 1:39–56, 2:36). The law made provision for women to make sacrifices, attend feasts, and make vows (Dt. 12:11–18; Lev. 27).
9. God has used a rod (Ex. 4:2, 17), ass (Num 22:28), ram's horn (Josh 6:5), ox, goad, nail, barley, cake, pitcher, jawbone, millstone (Judg. 3:31; 4:21; 7:13; 20:9–53; 15:15–19), mantle (2 Kings 2:8), ditches (2 Kings 3:16), empty vessels (2 Kings 4:3), cruise of oil, ravens (1 Kings 17:4, 4:6–7), cock (Mk. 14:72), and many other things to confound the mighty (I Corn. 1:18–21). Is it not possible then that He can use a woman?

Romans 16:1-2 – "I commend unto you Phoebe our sister, which is a servant of the church which is at Cenchrea: 2. That ye receive her in the Lord, as becometh saints, and that ye assist her in whatsoever business she hath need of you: for she hath been a benefactor of many, and of myself also."

Bible Commentary: Phoebe was known as a servant (the Greek word here translates "deaconess"). Her duties included providing care for female converts, preparing them for baptism. She visited those sick or in prison and managed all parts of the church work that pertained to the women that could not be done by the men. This provides evidence that women had important roles in the church.

Romans 16:7 – "Salute Andronicus and Junia, my kinsmen, and my fellow prisoners, who are of note among the apostles, who also were in Christ before me."

Bible Commentary: Paul refers to them as relatives, and some think they could have been husband and wife. We should note they were disciples among the apostles and were Christians. It is not clear where they were a fellow prisoner with Paul at.

1 Corinthians 11:3 – "But I would have you know, that the head of every man is Christ; and the head of the woman [is] the man; and the head of Christ [is] God. 4. Every man praying or prophesying, having his head covered, dishonors his head. 5. But every woman who prays or prophesying with her head uncovered dishonors her head, for that is one and the same as if her head were shaved."

Bible Commentary: In the phrase "the head of woman is man," head is not used to indicate control or supremacy but rather "the source of." Because man was created first, the woman derives her existence from him as man does from Christ, and Christ from God. Paul was addressing some excesses in worship that the women were engaging in here.

Submission is a key component in the functioning of any business, government, or family. God ordained submission in certain relationships to prevent chaos. It is imperative to understand submission is not surrender, withdrawal, or apathy; it does not mean inferiority because God created all people in His image and because all have value. Submission is mutual commitment and cooperation.

Thus, the Lord seeks submission among equals. He did not make the man superior; he made a way for the man and woman to work in unison. Jesus, although equal with God the Father, submitted to Him to carry out the plan of salvation. Similarly, although equal to man under God, the wife should submit to her husband for the sake of their marriage and family. Submission among equals is submission by choice, not force. We serve God in these relationships by willingly submitting to others in the church, to our spouse, and to government leaders.

<u>**1 Corinthians 14:34**</u>-35 – "Let your women keep silence in the churches: for it is not permitted unto them to speak; but [they are commanded] to be under obedience, as also saith the law. [35.] And if they will learn anything, let them ask their husbands at home: for it is a shame for women to speak in the church."

Bible Commentary: Is Paul saying that women should not speak in church service today? It remains clear in 11:5 that women prayed and prophesied in public worship. It all remains evident in chapters 12–14 that women are given spiritual gifts and are encouraged to exercise them in the body of Christ. Women offer much and can participate in worship service.

In the Corinthian culture, women were not allowed to confront men in public. Apparently, some of the women who had become Christians thought that their freedom gave them the right to question the men publicly. This was causing division in the church. Additionally, women of that day did not receive formal religious education as did the men. Women have been raising questions in the worship service that could have been answered at home without disrupting the service. Paul was asking the women not to flaunt their Christian freedom during worship. The purpose of Paul's admonishment was to promote unity, not to teach about women's role in the church.

Philippians 4:2-3 – "^{2} I beseech Euodias, and beseech Syntyche, that they be of the same mind in the Lord. ^{3} And I urge you also, true companions, help these women who labored with me in the gospel, with Clement also, and the rest of my fellow workers, whose names are in the Book of Life."

Bible Commentary: Two women, perhaps deaconesses, that had a differing opinion on some unknown point. Their broken relationship was no small matter; many had become believers through their teaching. Note: It is possible to believe in Christ, to work hard for the Kingdom, and yet have a broken relationship with others who are committed to the same cause. Although this happens, it should not remain broken long. We should be quick to repent and reconcile.

Barnes Notes on the Bible:

"I beseech Euodias, and beseech Syntyche" - These are without a doubt the names of females. The name Syntyche is sometimes the name of a man, but if these persons are referred to in Phil 4:3, there can be no doubt that they were females. Nothing more is known of them than is mentioned here. It has been commonly supposed that they were deaconesses who preached the gospel to those of their own sex, but there is no certain evidence of this. All that is known is that there was some disagreement between them, and the apostle entreats them to be reconciled to each other.

"That they be of the same mind" - That they be united or reconciled. Whether the difference related to doctrine or to something else, we cannot determine from this phrase. The language is such as would properly relate to any difference.

"In the Lord" - In their Christian walk and plans. They were doubtless professing Christians, and the apostle exhorts them to make the Lord the great object of their affections, and in their regard for him, to bury all their petty differences and animosities.

1 Timothy 2:11-12 – "Let the woman learn in silence with all subjection. $^{12.}$ But I suffer not a woman to teach, nor to usurp authority over the man, but to be in silence."

Bible Commentary: To understand this verse, we must understand the environment in which Paul and Timothy ministered. In first-century Jewish culture, women were not allowed to study. When Paul said that women should learn in silence and full submission, he was offering them an amazing new opportunity. He did not desire that the Ephesian women teach due to the fact they did not yet have adequate knowledge. Unfortunately, the Ephesian had a problem with false teaching (2 Tim 3:1–9) because they did not yet have enough biblical knowledge to discern the truth. Additionally, some of them were apparently flaunting their newfound Christian freedom by wearing inappropriate clothing. Paul was telling Timothy not to put anyone (in this case, women) into a position of leadership who was not mature in the faith (5:22). This same principle should apply to the church today.

Many interpret this passage to mean that women should never teach in the assembled church, commentators point out that Paul did not forbid women from ever teaching. Paul's commended co-worker Priscilla taught Apollos, the great preacher (Acts 18:24–26).

There are many women mentioned by name in Scripture. God chose to include them in His story of redemption. I have listed the scriptural references in which they can be found because I want you to search out and read their complete stories for yourself

Women of the Bible

- Abigail #1 – mother of Amasa, Sister of David. *I Chronicles 2:15–17*
- Abigail #2– wife of the wicked Nabal, became a wife of David after Nabal's death. *I Samuel 25*
- Abihail #1 – mother of Zuriel. (Zuriel was the chief of the house of Merari.) *Numbers 3:35*
- Abihail #2 – wife of Abishur and mother of Ahban and Molid. *I Chronicles*
- Abishag – concubine of aged King David. *I Kings*
- Abital – one of King David's wives. *II Samuel; I Chronicles*
- Achsah (or Acsah) – daughter of Caleb. When Caleb promised her to Othniel in marriage, she requested that he increased her dowry to include not only land but springs of water as well. *Joshua, Judges, I Chronicles*
- Adah # 1 – wife of Lamech. *Genesis*
- Adah #2 – daughter of Elon, the Hittite, and one of the wives of Esau. Possibly the original name of Basemeth. *Genesis*
- Ahinoam #1 – wife of King Saul, mother of Michal (wife of King David). *I Samuel*
- Ahinoam #2 – one of King David's wives, mother of Amnon. *I Samuel; II Samuel; I Chronicles*
- Ahlai #1 – daughter of Sheshan. *I Chronicles*
- Ahlai #2 – mother of Zabad (in David's guard). *I Chronicles*

- Aholibamah (or Oholibamah) – Daughter of Anah and one of Esau's wives. Also called Judith. *Genesis*
- Anna the Prophetess – aged Jewish prophetess who prophesied about Jesus at the Temple of Jerusalem. *Luke*
- Antiochus - a royal concubine who was given the cities of Tarsus and Mallus as gifts. 2 Maccabees
- Asenath – Egyptian wife of Joseph, Genesis
- Atarah – second wife of Jerahmeel. *I Chronicles*
- Athaliah – Queen of Judah during the reign of King Jehoram, and later became sole ruler of Judah for five years. *II Kings, II Chronicles*
- Azubah #1 – Caleb's wife. *I Chronicles*
- Azubah #2 – wife of King Asa, 3rd king of Judah, and mother of Jehoshaphat. *I Kings, II Chronicles*

- Baara – Moabitess, wife of Shaharaim. *I Chronicles*
- Basemeth #1 – daughter of Elon, the Hittite. One of the wives of Esau. *Genesis*
- Basemeth #2 – daughter of Ishmael and 3rd wife of Esau. *Genesis*
- Basemeth #3 – daughter of Solomon, wife of Ahimaaz. *I Kings*
- Bathsheba – wife of Uriah the Hittite and later of David, king of the United Kingdom of Israel and Judah. She was the mother of Solomon, who succeeded David as king. *II Samuel, I Kings, I Chronicles*
- Bernice - wife of King Agrippa Acts 25:13, Acts 25:23, and Acts 26:30

- Bilhah – Rachel's handmaid and a concubine of Jacob who bears him two sons, Dan and Naphtali. *Genesis*
- Bithiah – daughter of Pharaoh, Wife of Mered, a descendant of Judah. *I Chronicles*

- Candace – Ethiopian queen; a eunuch under her authority and in charge of her treasury was witnessed to by Philip the Evangelist, led to God and baptized. Acts
- Chloe - mentioned in Corinthians. Means "green herb."
- Claudia - greeted by Paul the Apostle. 2 Timothy
- Cozbi – a Midianite princess who was killed by Phinehas (grandson of Aaron) because her evil influence was seen as the source of a plague among the Israelites. Numbers

- Damaris. *Acts*
- Deborah #1 – nursemaid to Rebekah and later to Jacob and Esau. Genesis
- Deborah #2 - prophetess and the fourth, and the only female, Judge of pre–monarchic Israel in the Old Testament. Judges
- Delilah – the "woman in the valley of Sorek" whom Samson loved. Judges
- Dinah – daughter of Jacob, one of the patriarchs of the Israelites and Leah, his first wife. Genesis
- Dorcas, also known as Tabitha. Acts

- Eglah – one of King David's wives. *II Samuel, I Chronicles*
- Elisabeth – mother of John the Baptist and the wife of Zacharias. *Luke*
- Elisheba – wife of Aaron. *Exodus*
- Ephah – one of the concubines of Caleb (prince of Judah). *I Chronicles*
- Ephrath – second wife of Caleb (the spy). *I Chronicles*
- Esther (also known as Hadassah) – Queen of the Persian Empire in the Hebrew Bible, the queen of Ahasuerus. *Esther*

- Eunice – *Timothy*
- Euodia – Christian of the church in Philippi [1]
- Eve – first woman, wife of Adam. *Genesis*

- Gomer – wife of Hosea and a prostitute. *Hosea*

- Hagar – Egyptian handmaiden of Sarah, wife of Abraham. Hagar became the mother of one of Abraham's sons, Ishmael. *Genesis*
- Haggith – wife of King David, mother of Adonijah. *II Samuel, I Kings, I Chronicles*
- Hammolekheth – possibly rules over a portion of Gilead. *I Chronicles*
- Hamutal – wife of Josiah and mother of "ungodly" sons Jehoahaz and Mattaniah. *II Kings, Jeremiah*

- Hannah – a prophetess and citizen of Jerusalem. Mother of Samuel. *I Samuel*
- Hazelelponi (or Hazzelelponi) – daughter of Etam, tribe of Judah *I Chronicles*
- Helah – *I Chronicles*
- Hephzibah – wife of King Hezekiah and mother of Manasseh who undid his father's good works. *II Kings*
- Hodesh – one of the wives of Shaharaim *I Chronicles*
- Hodiah's wife – *I Chronicles*
- Hogla (or Hoglah) – one of the five daughters of Zelophehad who fought and won the right to inherit their deceased father's property. *Numbers, Joshua*
- Huldah – prophet. *II Kings, II Chronicles*
- Hushim – One of the wives of Shaharaim. *I Chronicles*

- Iscah – daughter of Abraham's younger brother Haran. *Genesis*

- Jael – Heroine who killed Sisera to deliver Israel from the troops of King Jabin. She was the wife of Heber the Kenite. *Judges*
- Jecholiah (or Jecoliah) – wife of Amaziah (King of Judah) and mother of Uzziah. *II Kings, II Chronicles*
- Jedidah – wife of wicked king Manasseh and mother of Josiah. *II Kings*
- Jehoaddan (or Jehoaddin) – *II Kings, II Chronicles*
- Jehosheba (or Jehoshebeath/Josaba) - daughter of

Jehoram and wife of Jehoiada. She saved her nephew Jehoash from massacre. *II Kings*
- Jemima – one of Job's daughters. *Job*
- Jerioth – wife of Caleb (son of Hezron). *I Chronicles*
- Jerusha – daughter of Zadok, a priest, wife of King Uzziah and mother of Jotham. *II Kings, I Chronicles, II Chronicles*
- Jezebel #1 – queen of ancient Israel. *I Kings, II Kings*
- Jezebel #2 - false prophetess. *Revelation*
- Joanna - one of the women who went to prepare Jesus' body for burial. *Luke*
- Jochebed – mother of Moses, Aaron, and Miriam. *Exodus, Numbers*
- Judith – Hittite wife of Esau. *Genesis*
- Julia - a minor character in the new testament. *Romans*
- Junia or Junias - Regarded highly by St. Paul in Romans. An apostle.

- Keren–Happuch – one of Job's daughters. *Job*
- Keturah – wife of Abraham after Sarah's death. *Genesis, I Chronicles*
- Keziah – second daughter of Job. *Job*

- Leah – first wife of Jacob who was given to him in place of Rachel whom he loved. *Genesis, Ruth*
- Lois, grandmother of Saint Timothy. *II Timothy*
- Lo–Ruhamah – daughter of Hosea and Gomer. *Hosea*

- Lydia of Thyatira – one of the first to convert to Christianity. *Acts*

- Maacah, the daughter of King Talmi of Geshur, was married to King David and bore him his son Absalom. 2 Samuel 3:3 [also spelled Maakah]
- Maacah - 2nd wife of King Rehoboam. Mother of Abijah, Attai, Ziza, and Shelomith. Rehoboam loved Maacah more than any other of his wives or concubines. "II Chronicles"
- Maacah #2 - sister of Makir, father of Gilead. Mentioned one verse later is Makir's wife, also named Maacah[105]. "I Chronicles"
- Mahalath – daughter of Ishmael and 3rd wife of Esau. *Genesis*
- Mahalath – granddaughter of David and the first wife of King Rehoboam. *II Chronicles*
- Mahlah – one of the daughters of Zelophehad. *Numbers, Joshua*
- Mahlah c *I Chronicles*
- Martha - *Luke, John*
- Mary – Mother of Jesus. *Matthew, Mark, Luke, John, Acts, Galatians*
- Mary – the mother of James and Joses (or Joseph). *Matthew*
- Mary – the sister of Martha. *Luke, John*
- Mary – the wife of Cleophas. *John*
- Mary – who was greeted by Paul. *Romans*

- Mary Magdalene – a disciple of Jesus. *Matthew, Mark, Luke, John*
- Matred – *Genesis, I Chronicles*
- Medium of En Dor - *1 Samuel 28*
- Mehetabel – daughter of Matred. *Genesis; I Chronicles*
- Merab – King Saul's oldest daughter. *I Samuel*
- Me-Zahab - mother of Matred, grandmother of Mehetabel. Genesis, I Chronicles
- Michal – daughter of Saul and wife of David. *I Samuel, II Samuel, I Chronicles*
- Milcah - wife of Nahor and daughter of Haran. *Genesis*
- Milcah - one of the daughters of Zelophehad. *Numbers, Joshua*
- Miriam – Moses' sister. *Exodus, Numbers, Deuteronomy, I Chronicles*
- Miriam – woman of Judah. *I Chronicles*

- Naamah – sister of Tubal-cain. *Genesis*
- Naamah - mother of King Rehoboam. II Chronicles
- Naarah - wife of Asher, tribe of Judah. *I Chronicles*
- Naomi – mother-in-law to Ruth. *Ruth*
- Noah – daughter of Zelophehad. *Numbers*
- Noadiah – prophetess. Nehemiah

- Orpah – sister-in-law to Ruth. *Ruth*

- Peninnah - wife of Elkanah. I Samuel

- Persis - a "woman who has worked hard in the Lord" whom Paul the Apostle greeted. Romans.
- Phoebe – a deaconess of the church of Cenchrea. Romans
- Priscilla – wife of Aquila and missionary partner to Paul the Apostle. Acts, Romans, I Corinthians, II Timothy
- Puah - one of two midwives who saved the Hebrew boys. Exodus

- Rachel – second wife of Jacob and sister of Leah. *Genesis, I Samuel, Jeremiah, Matthew*
- Rahab – of Jericho. *Joshua, Matthew, Hebrews, James*
- Rebekah – wife of Isaac and the mother of Jacob and Esau. *Genesis, Romans*
- Reumah – concubine of Abraham's brother Nahor. *Genesis*
- Rhoda – *Acts*
- Rizpah – daughter of Aiah and one of the concubines of King Saul. *II Samuel*
- Ruth – Boaz and Ruth get married and have a son named Obed. Obed is the descendant of Perez, the son of Judah, and the grandfather of (king) David. *Ruth, Matthew*

- Salome #1 – daughter of Herodias. Name in Hebrew reads שלומית (Shlomit) and is derived from Shalom שלום, meaning "peace." *Matthew, Mark*

- Salome #2 - a follower of Jesus present at his crucifixion as well as the empty tomb. Mark
- Samaritan Woman - (woman at the well) is a well-known figure from the Gospel of John,
- Sapphira – *Acts*
- Sarah #1 – wife of Abraham and the mother of Isaac. Her name was originally "Sarai." According to Genesis 17:15, God changed her name to Sarah as part of a covenant with Yahweh after Hagar bore Abraham a son Ishmael. Genesis, Isaiah, Romans, Galatians, Hebrews, I Peter
- Sarah #2 - wife of Tobias. Tobit
- Sheerah – founded three towns. Descendant of Ephraim. *I Chronicles*[184]
- Shelomit – mother of a blasphemer. *Leviticus*
- Shelomit – daughter of Zerubbabel, sister of Meshullam and Hananiah. *I Chronicles*
- Shiphrah – one of two midwives who saved the Hebrew boys. *Exodus*
- Susanna #1 - a woman who was nearly sentenced to death due to false adultery accusations before being saved by Daniel. Daniel
- Susanna #2 – a follower of Jesus. Luke
- Syntyche – Christian of the church in Philippi mentioned with Euodia
- Tamar #1 – daughter-in law of Judah, as well as the mother of two of his children, the twins Zerah and Perez. *Genesis*

- Tamar #2 – daughter of King David, and sister of Absalom. Her mother was Maacah, daughter of Talmai, king of Geshur. *II Samuel*
- Tamar #3 – daughter of David's son Absalom. *II Samuel*
- Taphath – daughter of Solomon
- Timnah (or Timna) – concubine of Eliphaz and mother of Amalek. *Genesis*[193]
- Tirzah – one of the daughters of Zelophehad. *Numbers, Joshua*
- Tabitha (Acts 9:36) – from Joppa, Tabitha was always doing good and helping the poor. AKA 'Dorcas'

- Vashti - queen and wife of King Ahasuerus. *Esther*

- Zibiah – mother of Jaosh
- Zeresh – wife of Haman. *Esther*
- Zeruiah – daughter or stepdaughter of Jesse of the Tribe of Judah, was an older sister of King David. Zeruiah had three sons, Abishai, Joab, and Asahel, all of whom were soldiers in David's army. *II Samuel, I Chronicles*
- Zillah – wife of Lamech and the mother of Tubal-cain and Naamah. *Genesis*
- Zilpah – Leah's handmaid who becomes a wife of Jacob and bears him two sons Gad and Asher. *Genesis*
- Zipporah – wife of Moses, daughter of Jethro. *Exodus*

Nameless Women in the Bible

- Cain's Wife- Genesis 4:17
- Seth's Daughters – Genesis 5:6-8
- Enos's Daughters – Genesis 5:9-11
- Cainan's Daughters – Genesis 5:12–14
- Mahaleel's Daughters – Genesis 5:15–17
- Jared's Daughters – Genesis 5:18–20
- Enoch's Daughters – Genesis 5:21–24
- Methuselah's Daughters – Genesis 5:25–27
- Lamech's Daughters – Genesis 5:2–31
- Daughters of Men – Genesis 6:1–8
- Noah's Wife, Son's Wives – Genesis 6:18, 7:1, 7, 13; 8:16, 18
- Shem's Daughters – Genesis 11: 10–32
- Lot's Wife – Genesis 19:15-26; Luke 17:29–33
- Lot's Daughters – Genesis 19:12–17; 30–38
- Potiphar's Wife – Genesis 39
- Shaul's Wife – Genesis 46:10, Exodus 6:15
- Pharaoh's Daughter – Exodus 2:5–10; Acts 7:21; Hebrews 11:24
- Daughters of Reuel – Exodus 2:15–22
- Daughters of Putiel – Exodus 6:25
- Wisehearted Woman – Exodus 35:22–29
- Tabernacle Women – Exodus 38:8
- Priestley Daughters – Leviticus 2:19
- Ethiopian Wife of Moses – Numbers 12:1

- Midian Women – Numbers 31:9
- Sisera's Mother – Judges 5:28-31
- Gideon's Wives – Judges 8:29–31
- Woman of Thebez – Judges 9:50–57; 2 Samuel 11:21
- Gilead's Wife – Judges 11:1–3
- Jephthah's Daughter – Judges 11:30–39
- Ibzan's Daughters – Judges 12:8,9
- Manoah's Wife – Judges 13, 14:2–5; Hebrews 11:32
- Micah's Mother – Judges 17:1–7
- Levite's Concubine – Judges 19:1–10, 20–30
- Four Hundred Virgins of Jabesh-Gilead – Judges 21
- Daughters of Elkanah – I Samuel 1:4; 2:21
- Tabernacle Women – I Samuel 2:22–25
- Ichabod's Mother – I Samuel 4:19–22
- Female Water Drawers – I Samuel 9:11–14
- Musical Women – I Samuel 18:6–9
- Abigail's Five Damsels – I Samuel 25:42
- Witch of Endor – I Samuels 28
- Daughters of the Philistines – II Samuel 1:20, Ezekiel 16:27, 27
- Mephibosheth's Nurse – II Samuel 4:4
- Woman of Tekoah - 14:1–20
- Ten Concubines of David – II Samuel 15:16; 16:22; 20:3
- Wench of En-Rogel – II Samuel 17:17–19
- Wise Woman of Abel – II Samuel 20:16–22

- Solomon's Wives and Concubines - I Kings 11:1–8; Songs of Solomon 6:8
- Two Harlot Mothers I Kings 3
- Mothers of Hiram – I Kings 7:13–15; II Chronicles 2:13, 14; 4:11-16
- Queen of Sheba – I Kings 10:1–13; II Chronicles 9:1-12; Matthew 12:42
- Wife of Hadad – I Kings 11:19,20
- Wife of Jeroboam – I Kings 14:1–17
- Widow of Zarephath – I Kings 17:8–24; Luke 4:25, 26
- Mother of Elisha – I Kings 19:20
- Widow and Her Pot of Oil – II Kings 4:1–7
- Great Woman of Shunem – II Kings 4:8–37; 8:1-6
- Wife of Naaman – II Kings 5:2–4
- Maid of Naaman's Wife – II Kings 5:1–19
- Mothers Who Ate Their Sons – II Kings 6:26-30
- Sheshan's Daughters – I Chronicles 2:34, 35
- Jabez's Mother – I Chronicles 4:9, 10
- Shimei's Daughters – I Chronicles 4:27
- Machir's Wife – I Chronicles 7:14,15
- Heman's Daughters – I Chronicles 25:5,6
- Artaxerxes's Queen – Nehemiah 2:6
- Shallum's Daughters – Nehemiah 3:12
- Barzillai's Daughters – Nehemiah 7:63, 64
- Women of Mixed Marriages – Nehemiah 13:23–29
- Job's Wife – Job 2:9, 10; 19:17; 31:10

- Lemuel's Mother – Proverb 31:1
- Zion's Daughters – Isaiah 3:16–26
- Virgins of Honor – Isaiah 7:14–16
- Isaiah's Wife – Isaiah 8:1–4
- Jeremiah' Mother – Jeremiah 15:10
- Zedekiah's Daughters – Jeremiah 41:10
- Wicked Hebrew Wives – Jeremiah 44:7–10; 15–30
- Women Who Wept for Tammuz – Ezekiel 8:13-15
- Ezekiel's Wife – Ezekiel 24:15–27
- Belshazzar's Mother – Daniel 5:10–12
- Southern King's Daughter – Daniel 11:6–9, 17
- Peter's Wife – Matthew 4:14-18; Mark 1:29–34; Luke 4:38–41
- Peter's Mother-in-law – Matthew 8:14–15; Mark 1:29–31; Luke 4:38–41
- Woman with Issue of Blood – Matthew 9:20-22; Mark 5:25-34; Luke 8:43-48
- Jairus' Daughter – Matthew 9:18–25; Mark 5:21–43; Luke 8:41–56
- Jesus' Sisters – Matthew 13:55, 56; Mark 6:3
- Herodias Daughters – Matthew 14:1–12; Mark 6:14–29
- Syro-Phoenician Woman – Matthew 15:21–28; Mark 7:24–30
- Wife Sold for Debt – Matthew 18:25; Luke 17:3,4
- Maid at Peter's Denial – Matthew 26:69–71; Mark 14:66–69; Luke 22:56–59; John 18:16,17

- Pilate's Wife – Matthew 27:19
- Women at Calvary – Matthew 27:55
- Widow with Two Mites – Mark 12:41–44; Luke 21:1-4
- Widow of Nain – Luke 7:11–18
- Woman Who Was a Sinner – Luke 7:36–50
- A Certain Woman's Message – Luke 11:27, 28
- Afflicted Daughter of Abraham – Luke 13:11–13
- Daughters of Jerusalem – Luke 23:28
- Woman of Samaria – John 4
- Woman Taken in Adultery – John 8:11; Deuteronomy 17:5, 6
- Hebrew Widows – Acts 6:1-4
- The Women of Antioch – Acts 13:50
- Daughters of Philip – Acts 21:8,9
- Paul's Sister – Acts 23:16-22
- Rufus' Mother – Romans 16:13
- Nereus' Sister – Romans 16:15

DIFFERENT SIDES OF THE SAME COIN

His lies and your excuses are one and the same!

I have no doubt that you have your own set of dreams, goals, and ambitions. And along with that list, you also have a list of excuses, like me, that are holding you captive. I've transparently exposed mine. But there are so many more. They are only limited by each person.

Your fate, like everyone else, and the distance between where you are right now and where you really want to be can be gaged by the number of excuses you make or the lies you choose to believe about your ability or inability to function in the beautiful world of endless possibilities God has placed before us.

The more excuses you indulge in, lies you believe and allow to detour your pilgrimage, the greater the distance and the longer the journey. We waste so much precious time trying to make God's plan fit into our limited understanding. I've said so many times that I just don't see it. Where is the money coming from? I do not listen to someone else's objection based on their marred thinking because of their own doubts and visionless mind. You know, "the dream killer."

Practically, everyone makes new year's resolutions at the start of the year. I'm sure you did too. But <u>only 8% fulfill their resolutions</u> by the end of the year. Most people only stick with them for less than 2 weeks. Talk about a short attention span. A total lack of commitment. We must change our focus and prioritize our actions.

For the most part, we were all born with two hands. But instead of being industrious, we waste time playing video games or just sitting around, twiddling our thumbs, watching other people on TV living a seemingly great life. We daydream about being but never put forth the effort. Almost every home in the USA has one or more TVs, computers, laptops, tablets, and smartphones. We have multiple opportunities to research and learn about almost anything, yet we use them to spend hours on Facebook or one of the shopping sites buying things that we can't afford. Imagine if you spent those hours taking a class on your interest, talking with someone who has excelled in the area you are interested, or praying to God for His directions in accomplishing your dreams. Most of the time, those things that we think are just our desires are the things that God has placed in us to accomplish. They most often are our place of joy, our means of resource, and gift back to God.

We have a brilliant one-of-a-kind idea. However, we continue to listen to the voices of the haters and naysayers telling us that it's been done before, or you don't have what it takes to make it happen. It may have been done before but, God will give you a new twist and a different audience.

No one person can reach everyone. God has enough people so that many can do the same thing, and everyone can still prosper. We tie our own hands and put straitjackets on God with our poisonous tongues and defeated thoughts.

If we make better time management decisions and use our resources better, we would have a great business, best-selling book instead of still just toying with the idea. Make the conscious decision to stop listening to and making the excuse and, instead, choose to hear God and make that leap. Leap with fear. I know the first thought is always "I'm already doing too many things. How can I fit one more thing into my day?" Well, my dear, all successful people, beginners and those with many years of success, have 24 hours. Don't have time? Find it. If not, make time. What's a few minutes, hours, or even days of discomfort when you have an expected end? Would you rather keep living like you are living, "stuck like Chuck" and unfulfilled, or give up some time and things now for something much better in the future? You're already discomforted living in poverty, choosing the same kind of bad relationships, or dead in jobs. What's a little more or different discomfort if it gets you to the desired end you are seeking? Our excuses are so familiar and comfortable that doing the right thing is overwhelming.

To EMERGE from the pit of self-defeat and destructive behavior, you must first believe in yourself before others will. Defeated even before you started. God gave each of us a message laced in the story and experiences of our lives that others can benefit from. One great service we can do for others is to share our mistakes in a loving way so that they do not have to make the same ones. Maybe you don't have to write it in a book, but you can begin to tell it to others as you interact with them during the course of your day.

If you are unsure where to start, talk to other successful people. Read a book or attend a conference. Make a plan or a draft. Just stop thinking and start creating what's on your heart; lay it before God, pray over it, and let Him lead you.

As long as you live, there's always going to be an abundance of excuses. In order for you to breakthrough and overcome them, you need to understand the anatomy of excuses.

Adapted from an article I was reading by Dominic Sohn on *Seven Things That are Necessary Knowledge About Excuses*, I offer the following thoughts for you to consider when trying to overcome the syndrome of excuse-making:

1. Excuses start off as good intentions to keep you safe or so the devil would have us to think.

Excuses usually begin as sound and rational reasons to keep you out of harm's way but can quickly turn into a destiny stopper.

"Don't talk to strangers" could be issued to you by your parents because they grew up in a rough neighborhood or had a scary experience as a child. However, this same statement can cause people to become housebound, afraid to venture outside the safety of their home for fear of being harmed.

Sure, avoiding contact with strangers might prevent you from getting robbed or mugged. But what if that stranger works in the company which you're dying to work for? What if that stranger is a potential raving fan of the good/service which you're trying to sell? What if that stranger could be the project partner, business partner, or life partner which you have been looking for all along, or perhaps they are the link to you overcoming that spiritual bondage you have allowed yourself to live under?

"Starting a business is very risky and requires a lot of money" might be screamed at you from a friend who got his hands burnt in business previously. People are well-meaning in their statements of caution. Most often, though, they elicit unfounded fears. They tell you it is much wiser to get another job or just keep that comfortable, boring job that you hate going to every day. Because, after all, all you want is to have the money to do what needs to be done; you don't have to enjoy it.

"Getting a job is your guarantee to a secure future" was imbued on you because your parents didn't have much to get by during their lifetime, and they don't want you to go through the same fate as they did. God never intended for us to depend on a job. Our only guarantee is in our trust and dependence on His provision. God is our source for all things.

Before we realize it, these well-intentioned reasons become excuses and stumbling blocks when: (1) the situation changes, and you don't have the drive or ability to adapt with the change; (2) they hinder you from accessing and unleashing your true potential.

Examine your reasons/excuses closely before accepting them. Is the safety of your current condition better than the rewards and generational benefits of taking that chance?

2. Practice makes perfect; unfortunately, the more you make excuses, the easier it is to make even more excuses.

It is so natural for us to look at what we think we don't have or cannot do. The more you do something, the better you get at it. This is the power of repetition.

When you make one excuse, it becomes easier to make another. After a while, they don't even ring out as an excuse but instead just a normal part of our flawed makeup.

On the flip side, when you overcome one excuse, it becomes easier to overcome another or to keep pushing yourself forward.

3. Turn your excuses is execution.

Think about that one thing which you really need or want to do; lose weight, traveling around the world, starting the business, reconciling with a loved one, having that conversation, etc.

Consider the myriad of excuses which you or others have been telling you:

- I'm too young; I don't have any experience it that.

- I don't really want this; it's too much work.
- I don't really need the extra money; I can just cut back.
- I'm too old; I don't feel like learning anything new.
- I'm not good enough; God can't use this mess.
- Others might laugh at me.
- I'm not experienced, qualified, or accredited.
- The timing isn't right.
- I'm scared.
- I'm worried it might not work.
- I'm worried that if it works, everything changes.
- I'm from a rough or disadvantaged background.
- I'm short/too tall.
- I'm not good looking enough.
- I'm shy.
- I'm a person of color.
- And on and on it goes.

The only way to push past and overcome the excuses is to execute. Get your mind and body moving in the direction you want to end up in. Just put one foot in front of the other, and don't stop until you get there!

Nike says, "Just do it." No more hesitations; no more later; no more next time. Move before you can talk yourself out of it.

Execution is defined as the carrying out or putting into effect a plan or course of action. It is not until you put action behind the plan that it has any validity—get beyond the thinking process and execute.

Another definition of execution is "putting to death," as in the execution of a death row criminal. Part of fulfilling your desires or the process of executing the plan should be the execution or "putting to death" of those things that are hindering you from moving forward. Put to death fear, excuses, procrastination, laying blame, and laziness.

As Shannon L. Alder puts it, "Before you can live, a part of you has to die." There must be a letting go of what could have been, how you should have reacted, and those words you wish you had said softer. You must accept that you can't undo or change past experiences, misguided opinions of others based on lack of information and failure to launch due to misplaced fears.

A good friend of mine preached a message, "Take Yourself Off the Hook." She encouraged us to stop holding ourselves hostage because the devil wants us to be in bondage, believing everything is our fault. She explained that he wants us to stay stuck, looking back and falling prey to our past mistakes. We must put to death those things that are not beneficial and hold fast to the truth of God's word. He can redeem us, no matter the size of the mistake.

You can get good at making excuses, or you can get good at execution; most of us can't do more than one thing at a time successfully.

You can wait for something to happen, or you can make things happen. I vote for making it happen. Consider this:

action or inaction. Either way, you are making something happen. So, why not make it count?

You can make excuses, or you can make an impact. We were all created to make an impact. It is no accident that you were born during the era you were or that you were born to those parents and live in that town. It is all a part of God's plan and your assignment. Assignments have timing, and they also have jurisdiction. We are most effective and impactful when we are operating where God has assigned us. Some gifts, blessings, and ministries have an expiration date on them. Once you let fear and excuses steal the appointed time, they lose the effect or desired outcome. God will even give the assignment to someone else if we fail to act when He calls. We are misinformed if we think He will wait until we are ready.

You can make excuses, or you can make money. So many people have died and taken their wealth potential with them to the grave because of fear. Fear is crippling, and fear causes poverty and destruction to our ability to make money. You can keep dreaming about living the abundant life God has promised us, or you can choose to make the necessary changes to your thinking and doing to activate your full possibilities, the inherent capacity of "EMERGING." Being all that God has deemed is you and yours.

Don't allow your excuses to be the only thing you are good at executing. The more you invest in making things happen, the more success, momentum, satisfaction, and fulfillment you will experience along the way. Momentum creates more momentum. After a while, the snowball will roll down the hill on its own because of the speed and momentum it has taken on from your earlier pushing and rolling. Same with executions; put in the work and time early on, and soon it will take on a life of its own.

Choices determine who you will end up being. Make a decision on which side you want to be on.

4. Others can make excuses for you, but only you can get over them.

It's not only us who can make excuses for ourselves. We're also influenced by others, television reports, and the environment; a number of things challenge our final decision or cause us to formulate an alternate outcome.

Despite the mix of excuses you might have on your plate right now, only you can get over them.

It is totally up to you on how you are going to respond to the excuse Kool-Aid. Stop drinking your own Kool-Aid, indulging in your own self-pity and thus self-destruction.

You can accept them to be valid, yield to them and convince yourself that the real you is out of your league. Or you could acknowledge those excuses, thank your friends and loved ones for their input (whether constructive or not), roll up your sleeves, and go to work.

Choose. Choose for you. Choose based on your desire and God-given giftedness. Only one life to live; only one life to give to His service.

5. You learn a whole lot about yourself when you dig deeper into your excuses.

If you want to find the root cause of a problem or issue, take it and do the 5 Whys Analysis. We've all gone through this process on our jobs. When there is a plan failure or accident, we have to go before the boss and explain what happened and how to prevent it from happening based on the 5 Whys.

The theory behind the process suggests that you should ask why 5 times, and you should arrive at the root of the issue or problem.

Excuse: I don't think I'm good enough to speak on stage.

Q1: Why do you think you're not good enough?
A1: Because I lack confidence when I have to speak in front of people.

Q2: Why do you think you lack confidence when you have to speak in front of people?
A2: Because I don't think I have the necessary skills to deliver a good speech.

Q3: Why don't you have the necessary skills to deliver a good speech?
A3: Because I've never taken the time to invest in that skill development.

Q4: Why didn't you take the time to invest in your skill development?
A4: Because I'm busy with other things.

Q5: Why are you busy with other things and not placing value on your skill development?

A5: Because I'm bad with time management, and I don't see my skill development as a priority.

Oooooooops, there it is!

From this simple example, we can see that it's not really a lack of communication skills that's stopping this person from killing it on stage — **it's a lack of the effective time management necessary.**

The deeper you dig into your excuses and really try to find out what's behind them, the more you will learn about yourself. We don't often like it when we realize that the only thing holding us back and keeping us from excelling or progressing is our lack of commitment to ourselves or the project that is demanding our attention. It is a real eye-opener when you come to the understanding that you are "sleeping with the enemy" of yourself. The one person you can never get away from. Self-defeating thoughts and actions or lack of have been the destiny destroyer of many people.

6. Making excuses is saying no to yourself and the situation even before you get started.

When you make and accept an excuse, the battle is already lost even before you set foot on the playing field. You have shot yourself in the foot even before the enemy has the chance to engage with you. It is awful to allow satan to have a victory he did not even have to show up to fight for. You have already turned yourself and the situation down, even when there's a chance that you could have really been awesome at.

When you think that you're not good enough to take on that client, you have already said no to yourself and to the client.

When you think that the audience doesn't want to listen to an old, fat, black lady like the devil kept telling me … Him telling me wasn't really the problem; the problem started when I began believing him. You have already rejected the audience and the opportunity; they might love a fresh, different perspective from someone like you or me. It is amazing how God can take the same seemingly old message and give it new life. How He makes it fit perfectly for every situation. You've heard it a million times, but for some reasons, coming from that person at that time, it suddenly has profound meaning and offers healing and peace.

When you think that your idea or opinion is stupid, you have already dismissed its value or possible benefit to others **even when there's a chance that it is what your boss, client,** or ministry is really looking for.

> **"Stop making excuses. Instead, excuse yourself and make something happen."**

So what's your next move? Stop making excuses and believing the lies; start taking action today! Remember that today is tomorrow's yesterday. Time is not standing still; it won't happen until you make it happen! EMERGE into you!

YOUR EMERGENCE

One definition of Emerge is to "move out of or away from something and come into view." In order to emerge into the people God has created us to be, we must move away from our old ways of thinking and doing and step into the view of new ideas and actions. Burst through that preverbal wall that is blocking you from the view of your purpose and destiny. That wall that has been a place of darkness, safety, and hiding. We cannot continue in the way we are and hope to find our true selves. Other definitions are to become apparent, important, prominent, to come out, come to light, enter the picture. What an awesome portrait of stepping into the life and position God has called you to. Your coming-out party is all planned; all it needs to be complete is the guest of honor. Kick a huge hole in that wall; march up to the door and step into your own celebration of life and destiny. No more listening to the lies; no more lame excuses. Tackle the fear; even better, "do it afraid."

Emerge!

"Rise" to the call.

"Come" out and make His plans known.

"Develop" into the image God designed you for.

"Begin" to walk in the fullness of your future.

"Materialize" the promises of God.

"Spring" into action.

"Show up" for your own life.

"Enter the Picture" and paint your own story.

"Arise" from the ashes of lies and excuses like the mythical Phoenix and take complete charge of you! Only you can prevent destiny-killing fires.

ABOUT THE AUTHOR

Barbara P. Hubbard is a wife, mother, and proud grandmother of three wonderful, beautiful grandchildren. She is most excited about being a woman "SOLD OUT" to Christ. She was saved at age 9 in her uncle Eugene's church in rural Long Island, VA. Although she has had membership at several churches throughout her life, the one thing that remains constant is her commitment to being an active member that intentionally leaves each job or function better than it was before.

She met her soulmate and life partner Leon at age 12 on the school bus. He asked her to marry him the next day. They married when she was 17 and have been married and best friends for 39 years.

She has a love for all things creative: sewing, crocheting, crafting, floral design, and home décor. She owned and operated Tifani Le'On Florist, a full-service florist, for 7 years. She has also been a full-service event planner.

She answered the call to ministry on December 3, 2017.

Her passion is for developing laden or dormant gifts in women of all ages, but most especially in aged women. She is currently the founder of Sisters of Strengths International Women's Ministries, an organization formed to provide assistance, training, and empowerment to women of all ages and walks of life. She desires to help women EMERGE into powerful forces for the Kingdom of God.

She is standing on the promises laid forth in I Chronicles 28:20. "Then David said to his son Solomon, 'Be strong and courageous, and act, do not fear, nor be dismayed, for the Lord God, my God, is with you. He will not fail you nor forsake you until all the work for the service of the house of the Lord is finished.'" This was a promise from David to his son Solomon that the God that had given him the assignment to complete the building of the temple would also, without any slack or lack, provide everything he would need. This included the laborer, money, time, and materials. He promised that God would be with him and would not fail him. This promise is still valid for us when we are on assignment for God. It is encouraging to know that we cannot fail because God will uphold us as long as we are obedient.

Barbara has been employed by the United States Postal Service for 22 years.

For speaking, preaching, or training engagements, contact:

Bhubbard3865@yahoo.com

Feel free to stay connected with Barbara Hubbard on Social Media at:

www.Facebook.com/Barbara.Hubbard.927
www.Linkedin.com/in/Barbara-Hubbard-41506487

RESOURCES

Meyers, Seth PsyD. *The Psychology of Why People Dislike or Hate Fat People.* Psychology Today online. May 6, 2011.

Jeremiah, David. *Women of the Bible, Her Story Part of History.* Davidjeremiah.blog. 2018.

Sohn, Dominic. *7 Things you Really Need to Know About Excuses.* Thrive Global.com. March 18, 2018.

Clarke, Adam. *The Adam Clark Commentary.* Spotlight.org 1832.

Clarke, Adam. *Women in The Bible.* Biblehub.com 1832.

John Barnett. *Discover the Book of Ministries.* Biblestudytools.com. 1998.

Elliott, Charles J. *Elliot Commentary for English Readers.* September 7, 2015.

Ross, Carolyn C M.D. MPH. *I See Fat People.* Real Healing 2013.

Henry, Matthew. *Commentary of the Whole Bible.* 1706.

Barnes, Albert. *Barnes' Notes of the Whole Bible.* Biblehub.com. February 1, 1983.

Richard, Randolph and O'Brien, Brandon. *Race and Ethnicity in the Bible.* July 18, 2013.

Mowczko, Mary. *All About Elizabeth in Luke 1.* MaryMowczko.com. December 16m 2017.

Bernardi, Patris S. *In Psalmum 90.* Biblestudytools.com 1839.

Gill, John. *Exposition of the Bible.* Christianity.com 2019.

Kennedy, Finetten Dake, Germaine, Annabeth Dake. *The Old and New Testament with Notes, Concordance and Index.* Lawrenceville, GA. 2001

Lockyer, Herbert. *All the Men of the Bible, All the Women of the Bible.* Zondervan Publishing 1958.

Life Application Study Bible. New King James Version. 1993.

Made in the
USA
Columbia, SC